MW00331441

南無本師釋迦牟尼佛

宣公上人德相

慈悲普度信者得救成正覺

過化存神禮之獲福悟無生

The Venerable Master Hsuan Hua

His kindness and compassion cross over all. Believers are liberated and perfect the Right Enlightenment.
Transforming beings wherever he goes, his spirit remains intact.
Those who venerate him obtain blessings and awaken to the Unproduced.

十法界不離一念心

The Ten Dharma Realms
Are Not Beyond
A Single Thought

十法界不離一念心

一九七二年宣化上人講於
美國加州三藩市金山禪

英　譯
佛經翻譯委員會
出　版
法界佛教總會
佛經翻譯委員會
法界佛教大學

The Ten Dharma Realms Are Not Beyond A Single Thought

Explained by the Venerable Master Hua in 1972
at Gold Mountain Dhyana Monastery, San Francisco, U.S.A.

English translation by the
Buddhist Text Translation Society

Buddhist Text Translation Society
Dharma Realm Buddhist University
Dharma Realm Buddhist Association
Burlingame, California U.S.A.

Published and translated by:
Buddhist Text Translation Society
Dharma Realm Buddhist University
Dharma Realm Buddhist Association
1777 Murchison Drive, Burlingame, California 94010-4504

First Chinese edition published 1996, Dharma Realm Buddhist Books
Distribution Society, as 十法界不離一念心 *(si fa jie bu li yi nian xin)*

Second English edition published 1976, Buddhist Text Translation
Society, as *The Ten Dharma-Realms Are Not Beyond A Single Thought*

Printed in Taiwan
First bilingual edition (Second Chinese edition, Third English edition)
1996

03 02 01 00 99 98 97 96   10 9 8 7 6 5 4 3 2 1

Notes: Pinyin is used for the romanization of Chinese words,
        except for proper names which retain familiar romanizations.

Library of Congress Cataloging-in-Publication Data

Hsüan Hua, d1908-
    [Shih fa chieh pu li i nien hsin. English]
    The ten dharma realms are not beyond a single thought : explained
by the Venerable Master Hsuan Hua in 1972 at Gold Mountain
Dhyana Monastery, San Francisco, U.S.A. / English translation by
the Buddhist Text Translation Society. — 1st bilingual ed.
        p.   cm.
    Includes index.
    English and Chinese.
    ISBN 0-88139-503-x (softcover : alk. paper)
    1. Buddhist cosmology.   I. Buddhist Text Translation Society.
II. Title.
BQ4570.C6H7613   1996
294.3' 42—dc20
                                                        96-19701
                                                            CIP

佛經翻譯委員會八項基本守則

The Eight Guidelines of
The Buddhist Text Translation Society

1. 從事翻譯工作者不得抱有個人的名利。
   A volunteer must free him/herself from the motives of personal fame and reputation.

2. 從事翻譯工作者不得貢高我慢，必須以虔誠恭敬的態度來工作。
   A volunteer must cultivate a respectful and sincere attitude free from arrogance and conceit.

3. 從事翻譯工作者不得自讚毀他。
   A volunteer must refrain from aggrandizing his/her work and denigrating that of others.

4. 從事翻譯工作者不得自以為是，對他人作品吹毛求疵。
   A volunteer must not establish him/herself as the standard of correctness and suppress the work of others with his or her fault-finding.

5. 從事翻譯工作者必須以佛心為己心。
   A volunteer must take the Buddha-mind as his/her own mind.

6. 從事翻譯工作者必須運用擇法眼來辨別正確的道理。
   A volunteer must use the wisdom of Dharma-Selecting Vision to determine true principles.

7. 從事翻譯工作者必須懇請十方大德長老來印證其翻譯。
   A volunteer must request Virtuous Elders in the ten directions to certify his/her translations.

8. 從事翻譯工作者之作品在獲得印證之後，必須努力弘揚流通經、律、論以及佛書以光大佛教。
   A volunteer must endeavor to propagate the teachings by printing Sutras, Shastra texts, and Vinaya texts when the translations are certified as being correct.

目 錄

Contents

Contents

開經偈
Verse for Opening a Sutra

無 上 甚 深 微 妙 法
The unsurpassed, deep, profound,
subtle, wonderful Dharma,

百 千 萬 劫 難 遭 遇
In hundreds of thousands of millions of eons,
is difficult to encounter;

我 今 見 聞 得 受 持
I now see and hear it, receive and uphold it,

願 解 如 來 眞 實 義
And I vow to fathom the Tathagata's
true and actual meaning.

十法界不離一念心

一九七二年宣化上人講於
美國加州三藩市金山禪寺

若人欲了知
三世一切佛
應觀法界性
如來唯心造

The Ten Dharma Realms Are Not Beyond A Single Thought

Explained by the Venerable Master Hua in 1972
at Gold Mountain Dhyana Monastery, San Francisco, U.S.A.

If anyone wishes to understand
All Buddhas of the three
* periods of time,*
He should contemplate
* the nature of*
* the Dharma Realm;*
The Tathagatas are made
* from the mind alone.*

若人欲了知，三世一切佛；
應觀法界性，如來唯心造。

「若人欲了知，三世一切人；應觀法界性，如來唯心造。」你笑我念錯了？是不是？

「若人欲了知」：若，是假設。人，就是一切的人。欲了知，欲了知個什麼呢？欲了知——人怎麼樣做人。

「三世一切人」：說「我聽說是『三世一切佛』，師父怎麼念成了『三世一切人』呢？」

人就是佛嘛！人，你叫他是「佛」，也可以的；佛，你叫他是「人」，也可以的。為什麼呢？人，可以成佛；佛，是人成的。所以你若說是「佛」呢？沒有人懂。「什麼叫『佛』啊？」沒有人真正知道。你若說是「人」呢，人人都知道是有個「人」。那麼知道有個「人」，就好辦啦，也容易了。

這個「人」是誰呢？就是「佛」。說那我是不是佛呢？你也是佛；他是不是佛呢？

Verse:

If anyone wishes to understand
All Buddhas of the three periods of time,
He should contemplate the nature of the Dharma Realm;
The Tathagatas are made from the mind alone.

Commentary:

"If anyone wishes to understand / All people of the three periods of time, / He should contemplate the nature of the Dharma Realm; /The Tathagatas are made from the mind alone." Are you laughing because I read it wrong?

If anyone wishes to understand. Suppose there are people who wish to understand how people become people.

All people of the three periods of time. "Shouldn't it be 'all Buddhas of the three periods of time'? Why did you say 'all people of the three periods of time'?" you ask. People are Buddhas. If you call a person a Buddha, that's okay; and if you call the Buddha a person, that's okay, too. Why is this? Because a person can become a Buddha. A Buddha is just a person who has realized Buddhahood. If you talk about Buddhas, no one really understands. "What's a Buddha?" they ask. Everyone knows what a person is. So we'll talk about people, and it will become easier to understand.

Who are the people we're discussing? The Buddhas.

"Am I a Buddha?" you ask.

5

他也是佛；我是不是佛呢？也是佛，卻是還沒有成的佛。成了之後，那是一個真佛，現在是個假佛。假佛也可以做真佛，真佛又可以做假佛。所以為什麼說一個「若」字呢？這個若，就是一個假設之辭，你不要那麼固執，把它看得那麼認真。所以說，假設你這個人，要明白、要了知「三世一切佛」。三世一切佛，都是人成的。

「應觀法界性」：你應該看看這個法界性。不是說那個法界的性，法界有什麼性啊？法界若有了性，那還叫法界嗎？這說的是法界的眾生性，眾生啊！各人有各性，你有你的性，我有我的性。說這個性，你不知道。你的脾氣就比我大一點，我的脾氣就比你深一點。你說是不是？不一樣的。

這法界的眾生，各有各性。豬有豬性，馬有馬性。豬，牠就姓豬；馬，就姓馬；牛，就姓牛。各有各「姓」，那是姓名的姓。這是性格的性，男人有男人的性，女人就有女人性，各有其性。那麼有的歡喜吃甜的，這是有個甜性；有的歡喜吃酸的，就有個酸性；有的歡喜吃辣的，就有一個辣性。啊！有的歡喜吃苦的，那麼我們大家就有一個苦性在這兒，你說是不是呀

You are.

"Are other people Buddhas?"

Yes, they are too. You are a Buddha, but an unrealized Buddha. After your realization, you will become a true Buddha. Now you are a false Buddha. False Buddhas can become true Buddhas, and true Buddhas can become false Buddhas. *If anyone wishes to understand / All Buddhas of the three periods of time.* The verse starts with the word "if" to indicate that this is only a hypothetical situation; don't be attached and think that it's real. The Buddhas of the three periods of time are just people who have realized Buddhahood.

He should contemplate the nature of the Dharma Realm. How can the Dharma Realm have a nature? If it had a nature, how could it be called the Dharma Realm? Actually, this refers to the nature of the living beings in the Dharma Realm. Every living being of the Dharma Realm has its own nature. You have your nature, and I have my nature. "I don't know what you mean by 'nature'," you say. Well, your temper is bigger than mine; and mine is deeper than yours. Thus, our natures are different.

Each living being in the Dharma Realm has its own nature. Pigs have the nature of pigs; horses have the nature of horses. Men have the nature of men, and women have the nature of women. Each has his or her own nature. Those who like to eat sweet things have a sweet nature; those who like to eat sour things have a sour nature; those who like hot, spicy things have a hot nature. Those who like to eat bitter things have a bitter nature, like all of us here.

7

？我們行苦行。一行苦行，這個修行也是苦行；到了過堂吃飯的時候，也是苦行。行那苦行呢，大家就都不要落到人後邊，要跑到前面去，那麼過堂那個苦行，誰都要跑到前面去，你看是不是？

你研究研究，各有各性。樹也有樹的性，花有花的性，草有草的性，各有其性，所以說「法界性」。不是說那個法界有性，是法界的眾生性。你們現在明白了沒有？以前你們都以爲是法界性，現在是那法界之中的眾生性，所以才說「應觀法界性」。

「如來唯心造」：本來說「若人欲了知，三世一切佛；應觀法界性，一切唯心造。」我因爲前面講「三世一切人」，現在最後一句，就給它改成「如來唯心造」。佛，就是由你心造成的。你心若是修佛法，就成佛道；你心歡喜菩薩，就行菩薩道，成菩薩。乃至於你心願意墮地獄，你就往地獄那兒跑，將來就墮地獄了。

[Note: In Chinese, the same character means both 'bitter' and 'ascetic.'] We cultivate ascetic practices. Cultivation is ascetic practice; even going to the dining hall to eat is an ascetic practice. When it comes to ascetic practices, none of you should fall behind. You should race toward the front. In the "ascetic practice" of eating, all of you race toward the front, don't you?

If you look into it, you'll find that everything has its own nature. Trees have the nature of trees; flowers have the nature of flowers; grass has the nature of grass. Each thing has its own nature. So "the nature of the Dharma Realm" refers to the nature of each living being in the Dharma Realm. Do you understand? Previously you thought that the Dharma Realm had a nature, but now you know this is referring to the nature of living beings in the Dharma Realm.

The Tathagatas are made from the mind alone. The original verse from the *Avatamsaka Sutra* said: *If anyone wishes to understand / All Buddhas of the three periods of time, / He should contemplate the nature of the Dharma Realm; / Everything is made from the mind alone.* I changed the second line to say, *All people of the three periods of time,* and I also changed the last line to *The Tathagatas are made from the mind alone.* Buddhas are created from the mind. If your mind cultivates the Buddhadharma, you will become a Buddha. If your mind likes the Bodhisattvas, you can practice the Bodhisattva Way and become a Bodhisattva. If your mind wants to fall into the hells, you are bound to fall.

佛法界

小來界台
不非世蓮
大去塵映
不非微交

The Dharma Realm
of
Buddhas

Neither great nor small,
Neither gone nor come,
In worlds as many
    as motes of dust,
They shine upon each other
from their lotus thrones.

不大不小，非去非來；
微塵世界，交映蓮臺。

今天還講這個十法界。第一個講到佛法界。這佛法界，我們到紅木城那兒去講過這個「佛」。我在那兒對大家就講，英文叫Buddha, Buddha, Buddha！我因為很愚癡的，耳朵也很聾的，就聽成一個「不大」。本來是Buddha，我說「不大」，這個「不大」是什麼？是佛。那麼有一個教授就很歡喜這個講法。所以講完了，他對著我合起掌來就叫「不大」。這個「不大」，就是沒有貢高心。佛就沒有貢高心、沒有我慢心。英文也有一個貢高的樣子，就叫「I，I，I」，佛沒有「I」。這「I」的中文就是「我」。我！我！我！我！我！什麼都是我，左右前後、上下四方都是我，這個我，啊！太多了。因為「我的」太多，就大了；佛呢，因為沒有我，所以就不大了。你聽這個講法怎麼樣呢？那麼小不小呢？也不小。若不大，可是他會小，那也不是佛了！那麼又不小，所以第一句就說「不大不小」。

「非去非來」：也不是去了，也沒有來；就是「來而未來，去而未去」。為什麼說非去非來呢？因為佛的法身是盡虛空、遍法界，無在無不在的，你若說他去，去個什麼地方？你若說他來，又來到一個什麼地方

Verse:

Neither great nor small,
Neither gone nor come,
In worlds as many as motes of dust,
They shine upon each other from their lotus thrones.

Commentary:

The first Dharma Realm is that of Buddhas. I once gave a lecture in Redwood City (California) in which I explained the word "Buddha." Because I'm quite dull and a bit deaf, when I first heard the word "Buddha" in English, I heard it as *bu da*, which means "not big" in Chinese. What is "not big"? The Buddha. One professor liked my explanation so much that when I finished my lecture, he put his palms together and said to me, "*Bu da.*"

"Not big" means not arrogant. The Buddha is not arrogant or haughty. An arrogant person is someone who is always saying, "I! I! I!" The Buddha doesn't have an "I," an ego. "Me, me, me"—everything is "me." Everything to the right, left, in front, back, above, below, and throughout the four directions is "me." There are too many "me's," and so the self becomes big. The Buddha, being selfless, is "not big." Then is he little? No. If he were little, he wouldn't be a Buddha. He is *neither great nor small.*

Neither gone nor come. The Buddha has "come and yet not come, gone and yet not gone." Since the Buddha's Dharma-body fills all of space and pervades the Dharma Realm, it is neither

13

？根本他的法身是周遍的，所以說非去非來。那麼是不是就在我們這個世界呢？不是。不是單單就在我們這一個世界。這個法界是所有微塵微塵那麼多的世界，無量無量、無邊無邊那麼多的世界，都是佛的法身。所以說「微塵世界」：像微塵世界那麼多。

「交映蓮臺」：交映，就是這個法界的佛這個光，照著那個法界的佛。那個法界佛的光，又照著這個法界。交映蓮臺，佛在蓮臺上坐著，互相放光動地，耳朵也放光，眼睛也放光，鼻子也放光，舌頭也放光，牙齒上又放光，不但這麼多的六根門頭在那兒放光動地，每一個毛孔上，都是放光動地的。每一個毛孔又現出來微塵世界，無量無邊那麼多的諸佛，就在那一個毛孔上，所現出來的。那麼每一個佛都是這樣子地放光，無量無邊的。但是和電燈一樣，你那個光也不衝突我這個光，我這個光也不衝突你那個光。不是說：「啊！你放那麼多光，我的光沒有地方了，這是不行的。」那光與光不衝突，光與光都是和的，這叫「和光」。所以，我們佛教就是和光的，這光與光不相衝突，我們人與人也不要相衝突，所以這叫交映蓮臺。這個交映，就是你的光照著我，我的光又照著你，光光相照，孔孔相通，和大梵天王那個網羅幢一樣的。帝網重重，無盡無盡，這就叫交映蓮臺。這是第一個佛的法界，是這樣子的。

absent nor present. You may speak of the Buddha as going, but to where does he go? You might say he comes, but from where does he come? Nor does his Dharma-body merely pervade our world; the Dharma Realm includes as many worlds as there are motes of dust—limitlessly, boundlessly many worlds—all of which are the Buddha's Dharma-body.

In worlds as many as motes of dust / They shine upon each other from their lotus thrones. The Buddha in this Dharma Realm shines his light upon the Buddha of another Dharma Realm, and the light of the Buddha in that Dharma Realm illumines this Dharma Realm. Sitting on lotus thrones, the Buddhas simultaneously move the earth and emit light from their ears, eyes, noses, tongues, and teeth. Not only do their six organs put forth light and move the earth, their every pore emits light and moves the earth. And in every pore, worlds as numerous as motes of dust appear, each containing incalculable numbers of Buddhas who emit light in the same way.

Yet all these lights, like those of many lamps, do not contend. One lamp doesn't say to another, "You can't give off so much light, because my light has nowhere to go." The lights don't clash with one another; they fuse together. In Buddhism, we unite our lights. Just as lights do not conflict with one another, so too should people not clash. We should allow our lights to shine on one another like the lights interpenetrating at the interstices of the infinitely-layered circular net canopy of the Great Brahma Heaven King. That's the Dharma Realm of Buddhas.

15

界法薩菩

悟埃行栽
覺塵萬培
情出度刻
跳六時
有情跳六時

The Dharma Realm of Bodhisattvas

Sentient beings when enlightened
Leap out of the dust.
Their six perfections and
ten thousand practices
At all times are nurtured.

有情覺悟，跳出塵埃；
六度萬行，時刻培栽。

第二個，就講到菩薩法界。方才爲什麼我把它換爲「三世一切人」？就是因爲這十法界都是由人修成的。人，不離現前一念心。所以第二個是菩薩法界。

菩薩法界，菩薩是梵語，翻譯過來，叫「覺有情」。怎麼叫覺有情呢？

這個覺有情有兩個講法：一個是覺悟一切有情，令一切有情都覺悟了，這是一個講法；第二個是有情中的一個覺悟者。

這兩個講法我們都有份的；什麼有份呢？有份成菩薩。我們因爲都是一個有情的眾生，我們也可以在這個眾生裏邊，做一個覺悟者。我們也可以以這個覺悟的道理，再去覺悟一切眾生。所以這個菩薩是不錯的，你也有份，我也有份。不單菩薩是這樣子，就是佛，我們也都有份。

「哦！我不明白這個道理，怎麼方才法師您說佛就是人成的！那麼我們爲什麼就不成佛呢？」不要說這個

Verse:

Sentient beings when enlightened
Leap out of the dust.
Their six perfections and ten thousand practices
At all times are nurtured.

Commentary:

The second Dharma Realm is that of Bodhisattvas. Why did I say *All people of the three periods of time* above? It's because people can cultivate to go to any of the Ten Dharma Realms. Yet people are not beyond a single thought of the mind.

The Sanskrit word *Bodhisattva* is translated as "enlightened be-ing" and has two meanings:

1. one who causes all sentient beings to become enlightened

2. an enlightened one among all sentient beings

We are included in both meanings. We all have a share of Bodhi-sattvahood because we are all beings. We can become enlight-ened ones among beings, and we can teach other beings to be-come enlightened as well. So being a Bodhisattva isn't bad. Not only do we have a share of Bodhisattvahood, we also have a share of Buddhahood.

"I don't get it," you say. "Dharma Master, you said earlier that Buddhas are just people who have realized Buddhahood. Well, why haven't we become Buddhas?"

19

「人成佛、不成佛」的問題，你說這個果方他將來會不會長大？果方雖然還是叫「小孩子」，那麼將來他會不會長大做一個人？做人又老了，會不會的？有這個可能，是不是呀？這就像我們現在是小孩子，佛就譬如大人，我們將來長大了就是佛，沒有長大就是小孩子。我們現在在佛教裏頭就是一個小孩子。啊！天天要吃奶，天天要聽法。這個聽法，是特別能增長人善根的，特別能開人智慧的。所以你若能有機會聽法，那比你賺多少錢都有價值。

所以我今天有一個規矩又要立出來，立出什麼規矩呢？我希望以後我們這兒的人，不要那麼多的 holiday（假日），不要那麼多的旅行，若放假的日子啊，以研究佛法做旅行，以研究佛法做 holiday；爲什麼呢？因爲 holiday 去旅行，太危險了。啊！你看看！每一個放假的日子，死的人，就不只一個，一定是多過一個。那麼多過一個，或者去旅行，就有份的。所以在這個國家，我們要矯正這個風氣。這個國家人人都願意玩，願意去旅行。我們佛教徒就要改善這個風氣。做佛教徒的不要去旅行，不要旅行那麼多。有這個時間來研究佛法，你說多好！來誦一誦經、念一念咒、拜拜佛，那更好！

拜佛是功德無量的，「佛前頂禮，罪滅河沙」，你佛

Let's not talk about people becoming Buddhas. Consider a small child who grows up, becomes an adult, and eventually gets old. We are like children within the Buddhadharma, and the Buddha is an adult. When we grow up, we will become Buddhas. But right now, we are still children in Buddhism. As youngsters need milk, we constantly need the nourishment of hearing the Dharma. Listening to the Dharma is an especially good way to make our good roots grow and to bring forth our wisdom. An opportunity to listen to the Dharma is more valuable than any amount of money you could earn.

Today I'm going to make a rule. I hope that from now on all of you will not take so many holidays and go on so many trips. Take the study of the Buddhadharma as your trip. Spend your holidays studying the Buddhadharma. Why do I say this? Because it's very dangerous to travel. Every holiday there are many fatalities, and if you travel, you might end up being one of them. We want to change the trends of this country. The people in this country are fond of recreation and travel. Buddhists should not take so many vacations. We can use this time to study the Buddhadharma. Even better, we can chant Sutras, recite mantras, and bow to the Buddhas!

There is infinite merit and virtue in bowing to the Buddhas.

Bowing before the Buddhas can eradicate offenses
As numerous as the Ganges' sands.

If you bow to the Buddhas, you can cancel as many offenses as there are grains of sand in the Ganges River. It is also said,

21

前拜一拜，你恆河沙的罪業都滅了。「捨錢一文，增福無量」，但是我可不是教你們捨錢給我，你們要明白。你們有錢，到其他的道場去捨去，那給你們增福是很多的。我們這個地方，因為我們都是苦惱人，受不了人的供養，若供養一多，我們或者就會死了。若沒有人供養呢？我們這個苦命運、這個苦生命，就多活幾天。你看！我們雖然苦，我們也願意多活幾天，不願意現在就死了。所以你要捨錢，願意捨錢，到旁的地方去捨去，我絕對是歡迎的。因為其他種福的地方多得很，不需要一定在金山寺。金山寺都是苦惱人，都是沒有福報的人，所以你們在這兒求福，是求不到的。你們不要害怕，我們餓不死！

「有情覺悟」：這菩薩是個有情者，有情中一個覺悟者，覺悟中一個明白者，明白中一個修行者，修行中一個實行者，這就是菩薩。所以說「跳出塵埃」：他若不明白，就跳不出這個塵埃，這個塵啊，太厚了，所以他跳不出去。你若覺悟了，這個塵就薄了，就好像塵土都沒有了，跳出這個塵埃。

跳出塵埃以後怎麼辦呢？是不是就睡覺呢？是不是就吃飯呢？不錯！還要睡覺，還要吃飯，還要穿衣服。可是怎麼樣呢？不是單單就做這些事情。本來你去做工，為著兩餐，為著吃飯、穿衣服、住，為衣、食、

"Giving a single penny brings limitless blessings." However, I'm certainly not asking for money from you. You should understand that. You can make contributions to other temples and earn great blessings that way. We here are so wretched that we don't have the blessings to receive offerings. If we accept too many offerings, we might die. If no one makes offerings, maybe we can live a few days more. Despite the suffering, we still wish to live a little longer. We don't want to die yet. Therefore, if you wish to give money, you can give it to other places. There are plenty of places where you can plant blessings; you don't have to do it at Gold Mountain Monastery, because Gold Mountain Monastery has only wretched people with few blessings. If you seek blessings here, you'll be disappointed. But don't worry, we won't starve!

Sentient beings when enlightened / Leap out of the dust. / Their six perfections and ten thousand practices / At all times are nurtured. A Bodhisattva is a sentient being; among sentient beings, he's an enlightened one. Among the enlightened, he's one who understands. Among those who understand, he's a cultivator. Among cultivators, he's one who truly practices. A Bodhisattva "leaps out of the dust." If he did not have understanding, he wouldn't be able to transcend the defilement. The dust would so thick that he wouldn't be able to leap out of it. When he becomes enlightened, the dust thins out and he can leap out of it.

"After a Bodhisattva leaps out of the dust, what does he do? Sleep and eat?"

Yes, he still sleeps, eats, and wears clothes; but he no longer works like a slave to provide his body with food, clothing, and a

住這三個問題；那麼你跳出塵埃，就不是爲這三個問題而生存了。那爲什麼呢？爲著要行這六度。

「六度」：就是布施、持戒、忍辱、精進、禪定、智慧。說：「我知道，這布施就是教人布施給我。」不是的，是我們要布施給人。所以那個錢，我們要揀開它，我們不要這個的。這一些個骯髒的東西，我們不要那麼多的。這個錢，是最邋遢的一個東西，你要是和它接近得太多了，那就是塵埃。什麼叫塵埃？這個錢就是塵埃。你能不要錢，那是最清淨了，就跳出塵埃了。你現在是跳出塵埃了，因爲你持銀錢戒。不過你不要再被它沾上。那麼這是六度。

「萬行」：再修行萬行。「時刻培栽」：不是說是今天我修，明天就不修了；今年我修，明年就不修了；這個月我修行，那個月就休息啦！今生我修行，來生就不修行啦！或者這一刻修行，那一刻又睡覺去了。不是的。時刻培栽，時時刻刻地都要修行這個六度萬行。不要說時時刻刻，就生生世世我們都要修行這個六度萬行。所以你能這個樣子，那就是菩提薩埵了。

說：「這是很不容易的！」你以爲做菩薩那麼容易就做啦？沒有那麼容易的。不單做菩薩不容易，做緣覺、聲聞也都不容易的。做什麼容易呢？鬼！做鬼最容

place to live. When you get out of the dust, you cease to be concerned with these three problems, and instead you concentrate on cultivating the six perfections: giving, holding precepts, patience, vigor, concentration, and wisdom.

"I know what the perfection of giving entails. It involves telling others to make offerings to me," some of you are thinking. Wrong. It is learning to give to other people. As for money, it would be nice to shred it up. We shouldn't want so much of that filthy stuff. Money is an extremely defiling possession, and too much involvement with it is what is meant by "dust." If you don't want money, then you will be extremely pure and will be able to transcend the "dust." Some of you have now transcended the "dust" because you are holding the precept of not handling money. However, make sure you don't get contaminated by money again in the future.

You should also cultivate the ten thousand practices and nurture them at all times. You cannot say, "I'll cultivate today, but not tomorrow. I'll cultivate this year, but not next year. I'll cultivate this month and take a rest next month. I'll cultivate this life, but not next life." To cultivate one moment and sleep the next moment won't work. At all times you should nurture your cultivation of the six perfections and ten thousand practices. Cultivate them in life after life. If you practice in this way, you will be a Bodhisattva.

"That's not easy," you say.

Did you think that being a Bodhisattva would be easy? Not only

易，墮地獄最容易，做畜生最容易，你若願意容易，就做那個東西去。所以你想要做菩薩，那就是不容易的；菩薩就叫不容易。容易就是鬼，不容易就是菩薩。說是：「很難的。」「難」也是菩薩，那個難，就是不容易的一個別名。

所以，菩薩就要行人家難行能行的苦行，難忍能忍的這種忍辱。人家認為很困難的，哎！沒有關係，我們去幹去，這個樣子的。不是說：哦！不容易做，我不幹了。你不幹了，那你就不是菩薩。往前進，精進！精進！精進！就是菩薩了，就是這樣子，沒有旁的巧妙的。你就是能做人家所不能做的事情，那就是菩薩。因為人人都不能做，你能做上來了，就是菩薩。

is it not easy to be a Bodhisattva, it's not easy to be a Shravaka or a Pratyekabuddha, either.

"Then what is it easy to be?"

It is easy to be a ghost, to go to the hells, or to become an animal. If you want things to be easy, you can be those beings. If you want to be a Bodhisattva, it won't be easy. You say it's difficult; the word "difficult" describes what Bodhisattvas do.

Bodhisattvas must be able to do what others cannot do; they must endure what others find difficult to endure. When people consider a job too difficult, they say, "That's all right; we'll handle it." They are not put off by difficult tasks. If you don't dare to do what is hard, you are not a Bodhisattva. Go forth with vigor! That's what a Bodhisattva is like; there is no other esoteric or wonderful secret. If you can do the things that other people cannot do, you are a Bodhisattva.

界　賢眠謝璟
法　聖獨秋連
覚　覺峯花二
緣　緣孤春十

The Dharma Realm of Those Enlightened to Conditions

The holy sages enlightened
to conditions
Doze high on mountain
peaks alone.
Springtime's flowers
wither in the fall
In a cycle of twelve
interconnecting links.

緣覺聖賢，孤峰獨眠；
春花秋謝，十二連環。

我們講這緣覺，因爲什麼我問你們這麼多的問題？因爲這個緣覺，就不歡喜有問題。他是孤獨的，不願意有其他人在一起。所以今天和你們研究這個大家共同在一起的問題——不要做緣覺。這個緣覺，在有佛出世的時候叫緣覺。沒有佛出世的時候，就叫獨覺，他自己就會開悟的。他就歡喜怎麼樣呢？「孤峰獨眠」。所以說「緣覺聖賢，孤峰獨眠；春花秋謝，十二連環。」這是講緣覺。講到緣覺，我們自己要「覺緣」，覺悟這種因緣。他是修十二因緣的，我們是十二因緣修的。

十二因緣，第一是「無明」。他觀察這個無明，無明從什麼地方來的？咦！很奇怪，怎麼會有無明呢？他就觀察了：無明緣行，有了無明，就有了行爲了，就有「行」了，有所表現了。有所表現了，就有了「識」。識就是分別，行就是個有爲法。無明那個時候，也談不到無爲，也談不到有爲。那時候就是在有爲、無爲之間，然後有了分別。

因爲什麼有了分別呢？就因爲有了有爲法。有了有爲法，然後就有了分別心。有分別心，然後就有了麻煩

Verse:

The holy sages enlightened to conditions
Doze high on mountain peaks alone.
Springtime's flowers wither in the fall
In a cycle of twelve interconnecting links.

Commentary:

Why am I asking you all these questions? Those Enlightened to Conditions (Pratyekabuddhas) don't like questions. They are recluses who don't like to be around other people. Today we are looking into the question of everyone being together, so you should not act like Those Enlightened to Conditions. When there is a Buddha in the world, they are called Those Enlightened to Conditions. When there is no Buddha in the world, they are called Solitarily Enlightened Ones, because they are able to become enlightened by themselves.

What do they like to do? They like to sleep in solitude on the mountain peaks. *The holy sages enlightened to conditions / Doze high on mountain peaks alone. / Springtime's flowers wither in the fall / In a cycle of twelve interconnecting links.* Speaking of Those Enlightened to Conditions, we should also become enlightened to causes and conditions. They cultivate the twelve causes and conditions. We, however, are cultivated by the twelve causes and conditions.

The first of the twelve causes and conditions is *ignorance.* They contemplate ignorance. "Where does it comes from? Strange! How

31

啦！這個「名色」就是麻煩。有了名色，一有了名，這就有「名」的麻煩；一有了色，就有「色」的麻煩。名色就是麻煩，麻煩就是名色。這個事情若講起來更麻煩，不講還沒有麻煩，一講就講出麻煩來了。說：「嗯！怎麼名色就是麻煩？我不懂啊！」你不懂？那你麻煩更多一點。因爲你有不懂的麻煩了，我沒有講的時候，你沒有不懂的麻煩。是不是？

我沒有這麼説的時候，你根本就不知道，你沒有這麼多麻煩。我這一講，啊！你不懂，有了不懂的麻煩。有不懂的麻煩，就想要懂了。這就有了「六入」了。你看，這六入就是想要懂，想要明白。聽過沒聽過啊？沒有人這麼講法！那現在就有了嘛！這就想要懂。

這六入就是想要明白才有六入。想要明白，於是乎，就生出一個眼識。眼根、耳根、鼻根、舌根、身根、意根，就生出了這個六入。這六入爲什麼要生出？就想要明白。誰不知愈想明白愈糊塗，愈糊塗愈不明白，這就是六入，就入了。你看！不明白，以後就要碰了。碰就是「觸」；各處去碰，東碰、西碰、南碰、北碰、上碰、下碰，就好像那個蒼蠅似的，各處去碰壁。爲什麼要碰壁？就因爲要明白。沒有聽人這麼講

can there be ignorance?" Then they see that ignorance leads to activity.

With the manifestation of *activity*, consciousness appears. *Consciousness* involves discrimination. Activity is a conditioned dharma, while ignorance is neither conditioned nor unconditioned; it is between the two.

Why are discriminations made? Because of conditioned dharmas. The discriminating mind is a result of conditioned dharmas. With a discriminating mind, the trouble starts. *Name and form* are the trouble. "Name" brings the trouble of name, and "form" brings the trouble of form. If I didn't talk about them, there wouldn't be any problems. Just mentioning them is asking for trouble, because you're bound to say, "How are name and form troublesome? I don't understand." Now you have the added trouble of "not understanding." Before I said anything, you didn't have that problem. Once I began talking, the problem of your not understanding arose and with it came the desire to know.

This quest for knowledge results in the use of the six sense faculties. See? The six sense faculties come into being because of the wish to understand. Have you ever heard such an explanation? No one has explained it this way before.

When you decide you want to know, the eyes, ears, nose, tongue, body, and mind appear. You think you can gain understanding through them without realizing that the more you want to understand, the more confused you become, and the more confused you are, the less you understand.

過，是不是？這沒有一定的法。怎麼講有道理就怎麼講，怎麼沒有道理也怎麼樣講。

這個觸就是個碰，到處碰壁。到處想要明白，誰不知碰痛了，就因為想明白。碰了之後，就有了「受」。「哎喲！我痛。」「唉呀！我很自在了。」我現在沒有碰壁，現在很舒服；一碰壁，就覺得很不舒服。沒有人說我一個不好，我覺得很快樂；有人說我不好，我覺得很不歡喜了。你看，這就是受，都是在這個地方，沒有在外邊，不要到外邊找去。

這十二因緣，講到「受」。受了，有了領受了就生出一種「愛著」來，就有愛著了。對於順的境界，就生出一種愛著；對不順的境界，就生出一種厭惡來。厭惡就不高興了！為什麼有個高興？為什麼有個不高興？就因為有一個愛，有一個惡。惡，就是個不願意、厭惡。所以這麻煩就一天比一天多起來了。

「緣覺聖眾，孤峰獨眠，春花秋謝，十二連環。」春天萬物發生了，這個緣覺的聖人在這兒就「春觀百花開，秋睹黃葉落」，他覺悟到這一切的事事物物，都有自然的一種生滅。所以他就觀這個「十二因緣」。

34

Since you do not understand, you seek *contact*. You go around making contact at random: east, west, south, north, above, below; like a fly madly bouncing off the walls. Why does it bounce off the walls? Because it wants to understand.

Contact is just bumping up against things, going everywhere bouncing off the walls. You go everywhere hoping to understand, but all that results from this desperate attempt is a lot of bruises. After the determination to understand sets in and encounters occur, there is *feeling*. "Ow, that hurts!" Or, "Ah, I'm so comfortable. Right now I'm not bumping into things, and I feel really good." But when you bump against something, you don't feel good at all. You feel happy if no one is telling you that you're not nice. But you get upset when you hear someone criticize you. This is where *feeling* lies; it cannot be found outside.

Once there is feeling, craving and attachment arise. You give rise to craving and attachment for pleasant situations, but you feel aversion for unpleasant environments. Happiness and unhappiness come from craving and aversion, and so every day the trouble grows.

The holy sages enlightened to conditions / Doze high on mountain peaks alone. / Springtime's flowers wither in the fall / In a cycle of twelve interconnecting links. The myriad things grow and prosper in the springtime, so the Pratyekabuddha sages contemplate and realize that everything undergoes the natural process of birth and death. They "contemplate the hundreds of flowers blossoming

35

前面講到這個「受」、「愛」。我們人爲什麼有一種不平安的感覺？就因爲有這種的愛。有了愛，就有了惡，也就是有了討厭的。那麼對你所要愛的東西，就生出來一個「取」了。怎麼叫取呢？就是得著，就想要得著了。因爲你愛，所以就想要得到。你得到了，這就滿自己的這種欲望了。那爲什麼要滿足自己的欲望？就因爲想要擁有它，所以取緣有，就有個「有」了。因爲有這個「有」，你想要得到屬於你自己的。啊！這一屬於你自己的，就有了「來生」。有了來生，又有了「老死」了。所以這十二因緣，就是緣覺聖人所修的。

in the springtime, and watch the dry leaves falling in the autumn." They contemplate the twelve causes and conditions.

Now we come to *craving*. The reason people feel unsettled is because of craving. Once there is craving, there is also aversion. You grasp at those things that you crave. What is meant by *grasping*? It means wanting to get hold of something. Because you have craving, you then want to obtain those objects in order to fulfill your desires. Thus grasping leads to *becoming*. Once you have these things for your own, there is further *birth*, which leads to *old age* and *death*. These are the twelve causes and conditions cultivated by Those Enlightened to Conditions.

聲 聞 法 界

聲 聞 眾 僧 男 行 權

不 論 女 觀 示

四 諦 實 隱

The Dharma Realm of Hearers

The Shravaka disciples,
Both men and women,
Contemplate and practice
the Four Noble Truths,
Concealing the real and
displaying the expedient.

聲聞眾僧，不論女男；
四諦觀行，隱實示權。

再講聲聞法界。聲聞，有初果的聲聞、有二果的聲聞、有三果的聲聞、有四果的聲聞。這裏邊又分出初果向——還沒有正式證得初果，叫初果向。初果、二果向、二果、三果向、三果、四果向、四果 。

聲聞的人，又叫阿羅漢，也叫羅漢。這羅漢，他能以飛行變化、有神通。證果的人，不是隨隨便便就說：「誰證了果了。」「我是阿羅漢了！」不可以的！因爲證果的聖人，他走路鞋不沾地的，你看他像在地上走路，但是他是在虛空裏頭，鞋不沾地，也不沾泥土。所謂不沾地，就是不沾泥土，甚至於在那個泥裏邊走，他那鞋子都很乾淨的。好像那個法順和尚斷流，他在很稀的泥上面走過去，鞋上也不沾泥，這是證果聖人的一種表現。不是說：「我證了果了。」就證了果了。

我的一個弟子很有自知之明，我問他證了什麼果了？他說：「證了水果。」證了水果，大約可以在水裏頭走，不怕水了。

聲聞，在初果要斷見惑；二果要斷思惑；三果要斷塵沙惑；四果也是斷了塵沙惑，無明呢，他破了一點，

Verse:

The Shravaka disciples,
Both men and women,
Contemplate and practice the Four Noble Truths,
Concealing the real and displaying the expedient.

Commentary:

There are Hearers (Shravakas) of the first fruition, the second fruition, the third fruition, and the fourth fruition. This Dharma Realm is further divided into (a) those approaching the first fruition, who have not yet realized the fruition; (b) those who have realized first fruition; (c) those approaching the second fruition; (d) those who have realized the second fruition; (e) those approaching the third fruition; (f) those who have realized the third fruition; (g) those approaching the fourth fruition; and (h) those who have realized the fourth fruition.

Hearers are also called Arhats. Arhats can fly and transform themselves, and they possess supernatural powers. One should not casually claim that he has attained the fruition, saying, "I'm an Arhat." That is not allowed. When a sage who has attained the fruition walks, his feet do not touch the ground. Although he appears to be walking on the road, he is actually traveling in the air. His feet do not touch the ground or the dirt. Even if he walks across mud, his shoes remain clean. Dharma Master Du Shun [the first patriarch of the Huayan School], for example, was one whose shoes weren't soiled when he walked over mud. This is the sign of a sage who has attained the fruition. One cannot casually claim to have attained the fruition.

41

但是沒有完全都破,沒有完全把無明都破盡了。這無明破盡了,就是成佛了。等覺菩薩還有一分的生相無明沒有破,所以就不能成爲佛。那麼四果聖人,他所修的是什麼法呢?他所修的這種法,人人都知道,我們人人都聽過,就是苦集滅道。

釋迦牟尼佛最初到鹿野苑度五比丘,就是憍陳如、馬勝他們這一班五比丘。這五個比丘,本來都是佛的親戚;可是跟著佛去修道,有的就受不了苦。釋迦牟尼佛在雪山的時候,一天只吃一麻一麥,餓得骨瘦如柴。那麼就餓跑了三個,說:「受不了苦了!」剩兩個。以後,釋迦牟尼佛在臘八那一天,天女送乳,天女給送牛奶去,釋迦牟尼佛把牛奶喝了,這兩個也跑了。這兩個跑,不是因爲受不了苦跑的,他們就說佛不會修行,說:「這修行要修苦行,要行苦行。你現在喝牛奶,這是不能修行的!不能受苦了!」也就跑了。這五個人一跑,都跑到鹿野苑去了。

釋迦牟尼佛成佛之後,先說了《華嚴經》,沒有人聽,以後就「爲實施權」,就說《阿含經》。要對誰說呢?一觀察:「我以前那五個同參,護我法那五個人,應該先去度他們去。爲什麼要先去度他們呢?因爲在往昔我發了這個願:我若成佛了,就要先度譭謗我的那個人、殺我的那個人、對我最不好的那個人,我

Hearers of the first fruition have eliminated view delusions. Those of the second fruition eliminate thought delusions. At the level of the third fruition, they eliminate delusions in number like dust and sand. The Hearer of the fourth fruition has partially, though not completely, eliminated ignorance. Only one who has completely destroyed ignorance realizes Buddhahood, for even a Bodhisattva at the stage of equal enlightenment still has a small amount of the ignorance of arising phenomena which keeps him from realizing Buddhahood. What Dharmas do sages of the fourth fruition cultivate? Everyone knows the Dharmas they cultivate; we've all heard them before. They are: suffering, the cause of suffering, the cessation of suffering, and the Way to the cessation of suffering.

In the beginning, Shakyamuni Buddha went to the Deer Park to teach those people who were to become the first five Bhikshus. This included the Venerable Ajnatakaundinya and the Venerable Ashvajit. These five people were, in fact, relatives of the Buddha. They had followed the Buddha to practice, but some of them couldn't endure the hardship. When Shakyamuni Buddha was cultivating in the Himalayas, he became as thin as a stick, because he ate only one sesame seed and one grain of wheat each day. Three of his followers found this unbearable and fled in hunger, and only two remained. Later, on the eighth day of the twelfth lunar month, a heavenly maiden offered some milk to Shakyamuni Buddha, and he accepted it. At that point, the other two followers left as well, not because they couldn't stand the hardship, but because they felt that the Buddha didn't know how to practice. They said, "You're supposed to be cultivating ascetic practices, and yet you drank milk. That shows you aren't able to cultivate

43

要先去度他去。」誰對佛最不好呢？你們有沒有人看過《金剛經》，《金剛經》裏談到有個歌利王。釋迦牟尼佛在因地做忍辱仙人的時候，他修行，這個歌利王就把老修行的身體給割了。爲什麼割他身體呢？

因爲釋迦牟尼佛在往昔修道，是個老修行；身上的塵土，修得也很厚，也不下山，在那兒用苦功、修苦行。那麼歌利王呢，他就帶著一些個宮娥、綵女、妃嬪，他這一些個太太、皇后都帶去了。帶去做什麼呢？到那兒打獵去。打獵就是打這些獐麅野鹿啦，打這些個東西。這一些個女人也都跟他去，但是女人就很好玩的，就不跟著他去打獵，到山上去，看見那兒有一個不知道是什麼的？因爲眉毛有三寸那麼長，頭髮有兩尺那麼長；臉啊，從來也沒有洗過，就好像塵土很厚的；衣服上塵土，最低限度大約也有一寸那麼厚。這一些個女人見到這樣子一個不認識的，就說：「啊！這是個妖怪！這是個妖怪！我們快走啦！」

這個老修行就說：「妳們不要走，我不是個妖怪。」

她們一聽，說：「咦！他會說話！」於是乎，有的膽大的就說：「你在這兒幹什麼呢？」

「我在這兒修行啊！」

and endure hardship." Therefore, they left as well. All five of them went to the Deer Park.

After Shakyamuni became a Buddha, he first spoke the *Avatamsaka Sutra*, which very few beings were able to understand. He then "concealed the true and offered the expedient teaching," and he spoke the *Agama Sutras*. "Whom should I teach?" the Buddha wondered. Then he recalled, "Previously I had five fellow cultivators who supported my practice. I should teach them first, because in the past I vowed that when I became a Buddha, I would first teach those who have slandered me, killed me, or treated me badly." Who had treated the Buddha the worst? If you've read the *Vajra Sutra*, you'll know about King Kali. On the causal ground, when Shakyamuni Buddha was cultivating as a patient immortal, King Kali had chopped off the limbs of his body. Why?

In that previous life, Shakyamuni Buddha was a skilled cultivator. His body was covered with a thick layer of dust and dirt, and he never went down the mountain. He remained there cultivating ascetic practices. One day King Kali took his concubines—his wives—along on a deer hunt. The women accompanied him into the mountains, but had no interest in hunting with the King. They wanted to have fun on their own. While strolling around in the mountains, they came upon a strange creature...they weren't quite sure what it was. Its eyebrows were three inches long and its hair was two feet long. Its face seemed to have never been washed, for the dirt caked on it was extremely thick. The dirt on its clothing was at least an inch thick. When these women saw it, they couldn't figure out what it was. They said, "It's a monster! Let's get out of here!"

「怎麼叫修行呢？」

說：「我修行想要成佛。」他就給這一些女人說法。

說了之後，這一些個女人就對他很有好感了，說：「啊！你在這兒太苦了，你都吃什麼啊？

他說：「我吃的就是草根、樹葉之類的，有什麼就吃什麼，我也不到下邊的人間去找吃的東西。」

啊！這些女人，時間一久，也就都不怕他了。這個去摸摸他的眉毛，那個又去摸摸他的手，那個又去碰一碰他的面，這麼樣子，就好像見到一個很心愛的什麼物件，就都想要接近這個老修行。

那麼歌利王各處去打圍回來了，找他這些個女人。一看，這些個女人都圍在那個地方；這歌利王就看看這些個女人都在那兒幹什麼的？他就走路很輕的，慢慢、慢慢走，慢慢、慢慢走，走到這兒一看，他這些個太太啊、皇后啊，和這兒有很奇怪的這麼一個人在講話呢！這個也摸摸手，那個也摸摸腳的，很不守規矩的樣子。啊！他就生出一種妒忌心了；在那兒聽聽，聽他講什麼。啊！說是講修行，在這兒講修道。

歌利王就發脾氣了，說：「你啊！不要在這兒騙女人了！你修的什麼道啊？」

Then the cultivator said, "You don't have to leave; I'm not a monster.

"It can speak!" they gasped. One of the braver ones asked him, "What are you doing here?"

He replied, "I'm cultivating."

She asked, "What do you mean by 'cultivating'?"

He said, "I'm cultivating in order to become a Buddha." Then he taught them the Dharma.

The women grew friendlier and expressed their concern, "You endure so much difficulty here. What do you eat?"

He answered, "I eat whatever there is—roots and leaves. I don't go out asking for food from people."

By that time the women's fears vanished. One of them reached out to touch his eyebrows; another touched his hands, and yet a third patted his face. They viewed the cultivator as something precious and tried to get closer to him.

Meanwhile, King Kali had finished hunting and was looking for his concubines. He found them all gathered around something and tried to see what they were up to. He worked his way slowly toward them, not making a sound, and when he was close enough he saw them talking with a very strange man. What is more, one was touching his hands and another was patting his feet! Seeing them acting so friendly, the King immediately grew jealous. The cultivator was talking to his women about cultivation.

47

老修行說：「我修的是忍辱。」

「什麼叫忍辱啊？」

說：「就是誰罵我、誰打我，我也不生瞋恨心。」

歌利王說：「你盡騙女人可以啊，她們相信你，我才不相信你這一套呢！你能忍辱？真的？假的？」

這個老修行就說：「當然真的了！」

「你說真的！我試驗試驗！」把身上的寶劍拔出來了，就把手給剁下來了一隻，說：「我現在把你手給剁下來，你瞋恨不瞋恨？」

這個老修行說：「我不瞋恨。」

「哦！好！你不瞋恨，你真有點本事，你盡打妄語，你心裏瞋恨，你口裏說不瞋恨，你來騙我！我是一個最聰明的人，你能騙得了我？」這歌利王又說：「好！你既然說你能忍辱，不生瞋恨，你那隻手啊，我也給你剁下來。」把那隻手也剁下。

剁下了，又問：「你瞋恨不瞋恨？」

這個老修行說：「還是不瞋恨。」

In a rage, the King bellowed, "You have no business cheating my women! What are you cultivating?"

The cultivator replied, "I'm cultivating patience."

"And what do you mean by 'patience'?"

"I will not become angry at anyone who scolds or beats me."

King Kali said, "You may have cheated my women into believing you, but I'll never believe you. You say you can be patient? Is that true?"

The old cultivator said, "Of course."

"All right, I'm going to give you a test!" The King then drew his sword and chopped off the old cultivator's hand. He said, "I've just chopped off your hand. Do you hate me?"

The cultivator said, "No."

"You don't hate me? Then you really have some skill. But you must be lying. You just say you don't hate me, even though in your mind you do. You're lying! I'm a very smart person. You think you can fool me?" King Kali continued, "All right, since you claim you are patient and don't hate me, I'm going to chop off your other hand."

After chopping off the cultivator's other hand, the King asked, "Now do you hate me?"

The old cultivator said, "No."

於是乎，他又拿著寶劍，把兩隻腳也給剁下了，這是剁其四肢。剁其四肢，又問：「你瞋恨不瞋恨？」

這個老修行說：「我還不瞋恨。不單不瞋恨，我若成佛，還要先度你。」那麼佛發這個願。當時天龍八部、護法善神就發脾氣了，就下大雨。這個老修行說：「我不瞋恨，有什麼證明呢？我若瞋恨你，我這個手、腳，就不能恢復如故了；我若沒有瞋恨心，我這個手腳啊，你雖然給我剁下來了，我還可以恢復如故。要是能恢復如故，像我原來的有手有腳，就證明我沒有瞋恨；我若有瞋恨，就不會這樣子了。」釋迦牟尼佛在因地，說過這個話之後，手腳果然又恢復如故。

這護法善神，一看歌利王這麼惡，把這個老修行四肢都給斷了，於是乎，就大顯神威，下雹子打這個歌利王。歌利王也知道厲害了，看老修行有這麼大的神通變化，於是乎跪到老修行面前求懺悔。

老修行就發願說：「我若不成佛啊，就沒有什麼可說的了。我若有一天成佛，我就先度你成佛。你若不開悟不成佛，我也不成佛。」因為這樣子，所以佛成佛了，就到鹿野苑去，先度憍陳如。這個老修行，就是釋迦牟尼佛；憍陳如就是歌利王。佛因為在往昔有這個願力——要度對他最不好的這個人。

The King then chopped off the cultivator's feet. Having hacked off the cultivator's four limbs, he asked, "Do you hate me?"

"No," said the cultivator, "not only do I not hate you, but when I accomplish Buddhahood, I will save you first. How can I convince you that I don't hate you? If I hate you, my four limbs will not be restored, and if I don't hate you, my hands and feet will be restored, even though you have completely severed them from my body. If they are restored, that will prove that I don't feel any hatred. If I feel any hatred, that will not occur." Whereupon the old cultivator became whole again.

Having witnessed King Kali hack off the cultivator's hands and feet in such a cruel manner, the Dharma-protecting spirits manifested their great supernatural power and pelted the King with a shower of hailstones. Realizing the severity of his offense and seeing the cultivator's great spiritual powers, King Kali knelt before the cultivator seeking forgiveness.

The cultivator said, "If I don't realize Buddhahood, there is nothing to be said. But if one day I do, I will save you first." That is why the Buddha first went to the Deer Park to teach Ajnatakaundinya, who had been King Kali in a former life. Because of his past vow, the Buddha first wanted to save the person who had treated him the worst.

After hearing this story, we should all vow that after becoming Buddhas, we will first save those who treated us the worst. We shouldn't think, "You've been so mean to me. I'm going to send you to the hells after I become a Buddha." Don't make that kind of vow.

我們聽見這一段公案，誰對我們愈不好，我們要發願成佛的時候要度他。不要「你對我這麼不好，等我成佛的時候，一定教你下地獄！」不要發這種願。

那麼佛到了鹿野苑，爲五比丘三轉四諦法輪。這第一次說法就這麼說：「此是苦，逼迫性；此是集，招感性；此是道，可修性；此是滅，可證性。」這第一次說。

第二次說：「此是苦，我已知，不復更知；此是集，我已斷，不復更斷；此是道，我已修，不復更修；此是滅，我已證，不復更證。」這是第二轉。

第三轉說：「此是苦，汝應知；此是集，汝應斷；此是道，汝應修；此是滅，汝應證。」

說完了這三轉四諦法輪，就說：「憍陳如，你現在在這兒被客塵來麻煩，你不得到解脫。」憍陳如一聽這「客塵」兩個字，他就開悟了。什麼叫客呢？客，就不是主人。什麼叫塵呢？塵，就是不乾淨的東西。我自性就是主人；自性是清淨的。所以他當時就開悟。開悟就叫「解本際」，就明白本來的道理了，成了「解空第一」。

When the Buddha went to the Deer Park, he spoke the three turnings of the Dharma Wheel of the Four Noble Truths for the five Bhikshus.

First he said:

> *This is suffering; it is oppressive.*
> *This is the cause of suffering; it beckons.*
> *This is the Way; it can be cultivated.*
> *This is the cessation of suffering; it can be realized.*

The second time he said,

> *This is suffering; I have completely known it.*
> *This is the cause of suffering; I have completely*
> *   eliminated it.*
> *This is the Way; I have completely cultivated it.*
> *This is the cessation of suffering; I have completely*
> *   realized it.*

During the third turning he said,

> *This is suffering; you should know it.*
> *This is the cause of suffering; you should eliminate it.*
> *This is the Way; you should cultivate it.*
> *This is the cessation of suffering; you should realize it.*

After the Buddha spoke the three turnings of Four Noble Truths, he said to Ajnatakaundinya, "You are troubled by guest-dust [transient defilements] and have not obtained liberation."

When Ajnatakaundinya heard the words "guest-dust," he became enlightened and realized the transience of defiling objects. "The

那個四諦法，要是研究起來，是無窮無盡的。今天時間也不等我了，也不等你了，也不等他了，我們時間又到了。

今天我們講「聲聞眾僧」，「不論女男」：這個證果，女人也可以證果，男人也可以證果，證果就是聲聞，就是阿羅漢。好像鳩摩羅什法師他的母親，就是證三果的聖人。

那麼「四諦觀行」：觀行，就是修行，觀察來修行。觀察修行什麼呢？修行這四諦法——苦、集、滅、道；知苦、斷集、慕滅、修道。要修這四諦的法門。

「隱實示權」：本來這一些個聲聞，你看他是聲聞，有的是大權示現，是大權教的菩薩來示現這個權教的聲聞，所以這叫隱實。隱，把這實在的功德他都隱起來了。示權，示就是指示，權就是權巧方便。你不要認為他是聲聞，是小乘，你就輕看他，不要這樣子。他這也都是大菩薩再來的；不是完全都是大菩薩，可是其中一定是有的。那這個大乘菩薩，他又現一個小乘的身，來接引這個小乘，然後迴小向大，所以叫隱實示權。這是聲聞這一個法界。

guest is not the host, and the dust is unclean. My self-nature is the host, and it is clean and pure." Ajnatakaundinya is called "one who understands the original limit." He understood the fundamental truth and became the "foremost exponent of emptiness."

The Four Noble Truths are infinite and inexhaustible. *The Shravaka disciples, / Both men and women.* Both women and men can realize the fruition and become Hearers, or Arhats. Dharma Master Kumarajiva's mother, for instance, became a third-stage Arhat.

Hearers *contemplate and practice the Four Noble Truths.* They cultivate the Four Noble Truths: suffering, the cause of suffering, the cessation of suffering, and the Way. This involves being aware of suffering, eliminating the cause of suffering, aiming for the cessation of suffering, and cultivating the Way. They cultivate the Dharma-door of the Four Noble Truths.

Concealing the real and displaying the expedient. You see them as Hearers, but in reality they may be great Bodhisattvas of the provisional teaching who appear expediently as such. This is called "concealing the real." They conceal their real merit and virtue. "Displaying the expedient" means they demonstrate skillful means. You should not write off all Hearers as Small Vehicle cultivators and look down on them. They may be great Bodhisattvas who have come back to the world. Not all of them are, but some of them are definitely Great Vehicle Bodhisattvas who appear among those of the Small Vehicle to urge them to turn from the small and go toward the great. This is called "concealing the real and displaying the expedient."

天法界

天　梵　欲　六
善　天　戒　五
因　十　有　種
難　漏　迴　輪
斷

The Dharma Realm
of Gods

*Beings of the Six Desire and
the Brahma heavens
Practice the five precepts and
the ten good deeds.
Planting seeds with outflows,
They cannot terminate
their transmigration.*

六欲梵天，五戒十善；
種有漏根，輪迴難斷。

我們今天就講講這個「六欲梵天」。第一個天是六欲天；六欲天就叫欲界天。欲界天、色界天、無色界天，這叫三界。

我們現在都在這個六欲天的四王天裏頭包括著。我們直接所看見的這個天，叫四王天，有四大天王管著。這個天是在須彌山的半山腰上。須彌山有一半是在人間的，在這四王天的上面還有一半。什麼叫四王天呢？是在須彌山東邊、西邊、南邊、北邊，這四大天王。這四大天王管著我們這個四天，一四天下；管著東勝神洲、南瞻部洲、西牛賀洲、北俱盧洲。詳細說起來，這是很多的，說不完。

那麼四王天的天人壽命多長來著？五百歲！他的五百歲不是我們人間的五百歲，四王天的一晝夜就是我們人間五十年。你算算這四王天的五百歲，是我們人間多少年？這四王天的天人的壽命是五百歲。以人間五十年做為四王天的一晝夜，你算算看，若三百六十五天，這是人間多少年？你們會算數的人可以算一算這個數目，這是四王天。

Verse:

Beings of the Six Desire and the Brahma heavens
Practice the five precepts and the ten good deeds.
Planting seeds with outflows,
They cannot terminate their transmigration.

Commentary:

Beings of the Six Desire and the Brahma heavens. First of all, there are the Six Desire Heavens, which are the Heavens of the Desire Realm. There are heavens in the Desire Realm, the Form Realm, and the Formless Realm—in all of the Three Realms.

Our world is located under the first of the six heavens of the Desire Realm—the Heaven of the Four Heavenly Kings. This heaven, which is directly above us, is governed by the four Heavenly Kings. It is located halfway up Mount Sumeru, which means that half of Mount Sumeru is within the human realm, while the other half is above the Heaven of the Four Heavenly Kings. The parts of this heaven located on the north, south, east, and west sides of Mount Sumeru are governed by the four Heavenly Kings, as are the four continents of our world: Purvavideha to the east, Jambudvipa to the south, Aparagodaniya to the west, and Uttarakuru to the north. If we were to go into detail, we would never finish our discussion of this heaven.

The beings in the Heaven of the Four Heavenly Kings have a life span of 500 years, but that's not the same as 500 years in our world. One day and night in that heaven is equal to 50 years on

59

第二欲天就是忉利天。這忉利天是梵語，翻譯過來叫什麼？不知道？就翻譯一個「不知道」好了，就叫不知道天。不知道天就是三十三，梵語叫忉利，翻譯過來叫「三十三天」。怎麼叫三十三天呢？因為帝釋在中間，這帝釋天是在中間住的。這個帝釋就是《楞嚴咒》上那個「因陀囉耶」；也就是天主教、耶穌教，他們所說的那個天主；中國人叫他玉皇大帝；在《書經》上叫他上帝——「齋戒沐浴，以事上帝」，你齋戒沐浴了，就可以侍奉上帝。

古來中國的人，不知道有佛，就知道有上帝。所以湯王的時候，他祭天就用黑牛來祭天，他就說了，「曰：予小子履，敢用玄牡，敢昭告于皇皇后帝。」皇皇，就是大的意思；皇皇后帝。「朕躬有罪，無以萬方；萬方有罪。罪在朕躬。」

他說「曰：予小子履」，商湯王他的名字叫履，他就說我小子，就是很客氣說：「我是很沒有用的一個小子。」一個小孩子的樣子。「敢用玄牡」，我敢用黑色的牛，「敢昭告于皇皇后帝」，我很至誠懇切地告訴大的上帝。說什麼呢？說「朕躬有罪」，說朕我一個人要是有罪，不要加到一般的老百姓身上去。萬方，就是萬方的老百姓。「萬方有罪，罪在朕躬」，一

earth. Figure it out: How many years on earth is 500 years in the Heaven of the Four Heavenly Kings? The beings in that heaven live for 500 years. One of their days is 50 human years. How many human years is 365 of their days? If you know math, you can figure it out.

The second heaven in the Desire Realm is the Trayastrimsha Heaven. *Trayastrimsha* is a Sanskrit word. You don't know what that means? Then let's call it the "Don't Know Heaven." The Don't Know Heaven is just the Trayastrimsha, a Sanskrit word that means "thirty-three." Shakra, known as *yin tuo la ye* (Indra) in the Shurangama Mantra, resides in the center of these heavens. He is the "God" revered in Christianity, and in China he is known as the Jade Emperor. The *Book of History (Shu-jing)* refers to him as the Supreme Lord and says, "Bathe and observe purity in order to worship the Supreme Lord."

In ancient China no one knew about the Buddha; they knew only about the Supreme Lord. In the Shang Dynasty, Emperor Tang used a black bull as an offering to the Supreme Lord and said, "I, Lü, but a small child, presume to use this black bull in venturing to make known to the Supremely Exalted Ruling Lord that if I have offenses, they are not the people's, and if the people have offenses, the offenses rest with me."

Emperor Tang's name was Lü, and he referred to himself as a small child out of respect for the Supreme Lord. He very sincerely offered a black bull and told the Supreme Lord that if he made errors, the citizens should not be blamed, and that if the common folk of

61

般的老百姓如果有罪了，那不怪他們，因為我沒有教化好他們，所以他們的罪都應該給我。

所以古來的聖人，他是這樣子，自己責罰自己，不是像現在的人，明明自己有罪，「喝！不關我事，那是他的，那是他的不對嘛，怎麼能怪我呢？」「你這個上帝，真是不公平，為什麼教他那麼有錢？為什麼教我這麼窮？為什麼教他那麼樣出貴？為什麼教我這麼樣賤？」這怨天尤人，什麼事情不說自己的不對，就找人家的不是。那麼古來的聖人哪，是認自己錯的。

所以這個帝釋天在中間，東邊有八天、西邊有八天、南邊有八天、北邊有八天，這四八三十二天，那麼這是第二欲天。

第三是夜摩天。夜摩天也是梵語，翻譯過來叫什麼？這個天上的天人非常快樂，一天到晚都唱歌。唱什麼歌呢？他就說他特別歡喜，說「快哉！快哉！」快，就是快樂；哉，就是：「啊！我快樂得很！我快樂得很！」晝夜六時他都是快樂的，所以翻譯過來叫「時分（匸ㄣ，份音）」，說每一個時分他都是快樂的。

第四是兜率天。兜率天，梵語叫 Tushita，翻譯過來叫「喜足」。他時時都歡喜，時時都滿足，這就是知足

his country committed offenses, the responsibility should rest with the Emperor for not having taught them correctly.

The ancients blamed themselves in that way, unlike people of today who clearly know that they are in the wrong but say, "Don't look at me! It's *his* fault! How can you blame me?" and complain, "God is unjust. Why does he confer wealth on others and make me so poor? Why does he bestow honor on some and leave me so wretched?" They blame heaven and curse mankind, looking for faults in others instead of admitting their own wrongs. The ancients acknowledged their own mistakes.

In the Trayastrimsha Heaven, Shakra resides in the middle, with eight heavens surrounding him to the north, south, east, and west, making thirty-three in all.

The third of the Desire Heavens is the Yama [Suyama] Heaven. *Yama* is a Sanskrit word which means "time period." In this heaven, the gods are so happy that they sing songs about their bliss day and night. They sing, "How happy I am! I'm so happy!" They are joyful throughout the six periods of the day and night. Hence, the name of this heaven is translated as "time period." Every time period is filled with happiness.

The fourth of the Desire Heavens is the Tushita Heaven, which translates as "happiness and contentment." The beings there are always happy and satisfied. Those who know contentment are always happy. That heaven is called the "Heaven of Contentment,"

常樂。他因為知足，所以常常快樂，所以又叫「知足天」；就是一天到晚也無憂無愁的，沒有煩惱，沒有worry（憂愁），這是第四。

第五叫化樂天，他會變化他的快樂。喜足，他就變不變、化不化，也都是歡喜知足，甚至於不快樂他也知足，總是知足。這化樂天，他會變化，能化出來這個快樂。

第六是他化自在天。怎麼叫他化呢？就是他自己本來沒有這個快樂，他能把其他天上的快樂拿來，做為他自己的快樂，所以叫他化自在天。這個天上有很多天魔在這兒，以天魔為眷屬。為什麼他要把旁的天上的快樂拿到他自己這兒來？就因為他不講道理。好像人間的土匪，多數都是化樂天的天人墮落，他到人間，還想搶人的錢，做為他自己的錢，那麼這是他化自在天。他把人家的東西搶來了，做為他自己的。這是六欲天。

梵天就是大梵天、梵眾天、梵輔天。六欲梵天，「五戒十善」：他們是修五戒十善所得的天上的福報。這五戒十善，都是有漏的善根，所以說「種有漏根」：種有漏的善根。他們寫著「種有漏因」，「因」也可

because the beings there never have a worry or care from morning to night. They don't have any afflictions or worries.

The fifth of the Desire Heavens is the Heaven of the Transformation of Bliss [Nirmanarati]. The beings in this heaven can derive happiness from transformations. In the previous heaven of "happiness and contentment," the beings are happy and content regardless of whether there are transformations; they are content even in unhappy situations. In this heaven, the beings bring about happiness through transformations.

The sixth of the Desire Heavens is the Heaven of the Transformation of Others' Bliss [Paranirmita-vashavartin]. The beings of this heaven haven't any bliss of their own, but they can take it from beings in other heavens for their own enjoyment. Many demons live in this heaven along with their retinues. Why do they take the happiness of beings in other heavens? Because they are unreasonable. Common thieves in the world of men are generally gods fallen from the Heaven of the Transformation of Others' Bliss. Having fallen, they still have the habit of stealing money from others.

The Brahma Heavens include the Great Brahma [Mahabrahma] Heaven, the Multitudes of Brahma [Brahmakayika] Heaven, and the Ministers of Brahma [Brahmapurohita] Heaven. Beings of the Six Desire Heavens and the Brahma Heavens *practice the five precepts and the ten good deeds.* Because these beings cultivated the five precepts and the ten good deeds, they obtain the blessings and rewards of the heavens. However, the cultivation of the five

以，種有漏的因。「豈有他焉」，旁人管不了的，這都自己去的。

講經說法是不容易的，我現在因為沒有想就說出來了，有人又說了，說：「師父講錯了！」在心裏這麼樣說，口裏不敢講。但是我這個人也很怪的，你在心裏一說，我這兒電報就打來了，所以要把它改了。「輪迴難斷」是不是啊？這回對了嗎？是你心裏說我講錯了，是不是？（弟子：是。）不是一個人這麼樣想，還有，趕快自己說出來，是誰這麼樣想來著？要坦白！若不坦白，那就永遠不會成道的。

precepts and the ten good deeds plants good roots that have out-flows, so the verse says: *Planting seeds with outflows. / It has nothing to do with anyone else at all.* [Note: This last line is actually from the verse for the Dharma Realm of People.] You yourself are responsible.

It's not easy to explain the Sutras. I don't prepare ahead of time for my lectures. Some of you are thinking that I said the verse wrong, but you don't dare to say it aloud. Strangely enough, though, once you say it in your mind, I receive your telegram. So I'll correct the last line: *They cannot terminate their transmigration.* Am I right this time? Did you think to yourselves that I said it wrong? [Disciple: "Yes."] More than one of you thought that way. The rest of you should also admit to having such thoughts. Be honest. If you aren't honest, you will never attain the Way.

阿修羅法界

暴擽狠牽
性無鬥業
羅福勇沉
修有好浮

The Dharma Realm
of
Asuras

Asuras have a violent nature,
Laden with blessings,
  lacking power.
Absolutely determined
  to fight,
They bob along
  in karma's tow.

修羅性暴，有福無權；
好勇鬥狠，浮沉業牽。

阿修羅是梵語，翻譯過來叫「無端正」，無端正就是醜陋。可是醜陋，是這個男的阿修羅，相貌非常醜陋；女的阿修羅，相貌又非常地美麗。男的阿修羅，他其性好鬥，是在外邊的鬥爭，向外鬥爭；女的阿修羅，其性也是好鬥爭，但是她在裏邊鬥爭，不是在外邊鬥爭。怎麼在裏邊鬥爭呢？她用心來鬥爭，也就是所謂的妒忌障礙、無明煩惱都在裏邊。

這一類的眾生，有的時候把他論到三善道裏邊，就是天、人、阿修羅這三善道；有的時候又把他放到四惡趣裏邊，就是地獄、餓鬼、畜生、阿修羅，這叫四惡趣。

這阿修羅，畜生裏邊也有阿修羅，人道裏邊也有阿修羅，天道裏邊也有阿修羅，鬼道裏邊也有阿修羅。所以阿修羅自己是一個法界，但是又通於其他三法界，所以在這四道裏頭，都有阿修羅。總而言之，無論在哪一個道裏邊，他是好鬥爭的，他脾氣非常大，好說了算。說了算，就是他願意做 boss（老闆），願意指揮其他的人，不願意受其他的人指揮；願意管著其他

Verse:

Asuras have a violent nature,
Laden with blessings, lacking power.
Absolutely determined to fight,
They bob along in karma's tow.

Commentary:

Asura is a Sanskrit word that means "ugly." Male asuras are extremely ugly; the females are beautiful. It is the nature of the male asura to initiate fights. The female asura is also naturally fond of fighting, but wages covert wars, unlike the overt physical battles of the males, using weapons of the mind such as jealousy, obstructiveness, ignorance, and affliction.

Sometimes this realm is included in the Three Good Realms—gods, humans, and asuras. At other times they are classified as one of the Four Evil Realms—hell-beings, hungry ghosts, animals, and asuras.

There are asuras in the animal realm, in the human realm, in the heavens, and among the hungry ghosts. Although the asuras are an individual Dharma Realm by themselves, they appear in the other realms as well. In general, regardless of what realm they are in, they like to pick fights, and they have bad tempers. They enjoy bossing others around and like to be supervisors, but they can't stand supervision. They won't be controlled by others. These are the characteristics of asuras.

71

的人，不願意受其他人的管，這都是修羅的表現。

這修羅，你們沒有看見，我可以告訴你們。修羅又有善的阿修羅，又有惡的阿修羅。善的阿修羅，就是國家的軍隊、兵、將軍，這都是阿修羅；惡的阿修羅，不善的阿修羅，就是土匪、小偷，偷人東西、強搶人東西這種，好打人這一類的人，好殺人這一類的人，這都叫阿修羅。這是在人道上，我們都看得見的。

天上也有這一類的阿修羅。在天上的阿修羅，他和天兵、天將去作戰，一天到晚，想要搶帝釋天這個寶座，想要把帝釋天給打倒了，他去做帝釋天。可是他戰來戰去，總要失敗的。為什麼呢？因為他有天福沒有天權；他可以在天上享受這個天福，但是他不能有權力，所以他雖然和天兵、天將作戰，始終是失敗的。這是人間的阿修羅和天上的阿修羅。

畜生怎麼又有阿修羅呢？畜生阿修羅，好像老虎，這是畜生裏頭的阿修羅；獅子，這是畜生裏頭的阿修羅；豺狼，這是畜生裏頭的阿修羅。那麼這類阿修羅，牠就願意欺負其他的同類，欺負其他的畜生，就好像那個狼啊、虎啊、老虎、獅子，都想吃其他的畜生。為什麼牠要吃其他的畜生呢？就因為牠是一種修羅性。還有蛇、飛禽裏邊那個鷹，這都是阿修羅。

If you haven't noticed the asuras, I can tell you more about them. Among people, asuras can be good or bad. The good asuras include military officials and troops, and bad asuras are bandits, thieves, robbers, thugs, murderers, and the like. We can see these asuras in the world of men.

There are also asuras in the heavens. Heavenly asuras wage battles against the heavenly troops of Shakra. From morning to night, they attempt to overthrow Shakra so that they can seize his jeweled throne and become the heavenly king. But no matter what strategy they use, they are always defeated, because they are "laden with blessings, lacking power." They have accumulated the blessings that earn them rebirth in the heavens, but they have no authority there. For that reason, they are invariably defeated in their battles with the heavenly troops.

Are there asuras in the animal realm? Yes. Tigers, for instance, are asuras among the animals. Lions and wolves are also asuras among the animals. These asuras bully the other animals. Wolves, tigers, and lions kill other animals for food. They prey on other animals because they have the nature of asuras. Snakes and eagles are also asuras.

In general, asuras are utterly unreasonable and have huge tempers. They are constantly blowing their tops. Too much temper!

There are also asuras in the hungry ghost realm, and they go around bullying other ghosts. The realm of hungry ghosts has kind

總而言之，阿修羅就是不講道理，他脾氣大，無論對任何人，他常常要發脾氣。 Too much temper！（太多脾氣了！）那麼這畜生裏頭的阿修羅，是這樣子。鬼裏頭也有阿修羅，這種阿修羅，他就欺負其他的鬼。

鬼裏頭也有善鬼、有惡鬼。這惡鬼在鬼裏頭，也不講道理。本來鬼就是不講道理的，他在不講道理的裏邊，還更不講道理！所以說「修羅性暴」：他的性非常暴躁。

「有福無權」：他是有天福而沒有天權的眾生。他想要爭權奪利，但是也爭不到。「好勇鬥狠」：他好和人作戰，好和人鬥爭。現在你看這個世界，都是修羅世界，都講鬥爭、鬥爭；鬥爭這個，鬥爭那個，你把我鬥倒了，我把你鬥臭了。

你看，在中國那個林彪就是豺狼轉世，所以他那麼惡，百萬大軍他都可以帶，有方法把他們都管得服服貼貼的。周恩來是個人，周恩來不單是個人，而且還是一個非常非常聰明的人，比諸葛亮都聰明，所以他在這麼壞的一個世界上，他還能立得住，這是我告訴你們。

前五、六年，我就告訴你們這個祕密，不過你們都不注意。有人現在就問了，說：「您知道林彪是豺狼，

ghosts and evil ghosts. Evil ghosts are utterly unreasonable. Ghosts are not reasonable to begin with, but these asura ghosts are even more unreasonable. And so the verse says: *Asuras have a violent nature.* They have explosive tempers.

Laden with blessings, lacking power. They have heavenly blessings, but lack heavenly authority. They fight for power and advantages, but fail to obtain them. *Absolutely determined to fight:* they love to fight and wage war. The modern world is a world of asuras—everyone is fighting and struggling, trying to knock each other down.

China's Lin Biao [Mao Zedong's successor] was a wolf in a previous life; that's why he was so evil. He could lead an army of millions of soldiers. He knew the ways to tame them and make them obedient. Zhou Enlai was a human being in his past life, and a very intelligent one at that. He was even smarter than Zhu Geliang [the brilliant strategist in the Three Kingdoms era]. That's why he was able to stand firm in such a tumultuous world.

I told you these secrets five or six years ago, but none of you paid any attention. "You say that Lin Biao was a wolf. What about Zhu De [senior vice-chairman of the Chinese Communist Party when Mao was the chairman]?" someone asks. Zhu De was a lion. Someone else asks, "Then what was I?" You're just you, and I'm just me. I'm talking about famous people in the world. You aren't famous, so you don't get a turn.

朱德是個什麼呢？」那麼有人說：「那我是個什麼呢
？」你就是個你，我就是個我。因為我所說的這是世
界最有名的人，我說一說；沒有名的人還談不到，還
輪不到你。

所以這都是修羅，他們都好勇鬥狠，就鬥爭、鬥爭，
鬥爭一百年，鬥爭二百年，鬥爭三百年，鬥爭五百年
，鬥爭一千年。你看他這種的理論，鬥爭要鬥爭到一
千年去。唉！佛法所以到這鬥爭堅固的時候，是末法
時代。

但是，我們大家要發願：「我們不要末法，我們就要
正法！我們走到什麼地方，什麼地方就要變成正法！
」我們發這個願，就是在末法時代，我們若到哪個地
方，哪個地方就要變成正法。那麼人人發這個願，人
人就都滿這個願。到這個末法時代把它變成正法，這
就叫天翻地覆，把天地都給它翻過來。它是這樣子嗎
？我們不教它這樣子。

「浮沉業牽」：這阿修羅，他或者生天，或者在人道
，或者在畜生道，或者在餓鬼道，都是由著業力牽引
著他，才起惑、造業、受報，就在這個地方，就受這
種的果報。所以說浮沉業牽，由他業力牽引著到哪一
道裏頭去。所以人修行，切記不要和人鬥爭，不要好
勇鬥狠，不要性暴，那麼就和修羅脫離關係了。

Asuras are so belligerent that they can keep fighting for one hundred, two hundred, three hundred, five hundred, or even a thousand years. They could fight for a thousand years without getting tired of it!

This is the Age Strong in Fighting and also the Dharma-ending Age. Nevertheless, we don't want it to be the Dharma-ending Age; we want the Proper Dharma to prevail. We should vow that wherever we go, the Proper Dharma will prevail. If we do that, every place we go will become a place of genuine Dharma. If everyone fulfilled this vow, the Dharma-ending Age would become the Proper Dharma Age. We can turn the situation around.

They bob along in karma's tow. Asuras may be born in the heavens, in the human realm, or in the realms of animals and hungry ghosts. Dragged by the force of their karma, they become deluded, create more karma, and undergo the retribution. The force of their karma pulls them to undergo retribution in various realms. Cultivators should take care not to be belligerent and hot-tempered. Then they won't get dragged into the asura realm.

If we study them in detail, we find that there are asuras in five of the nine Dharma Realms of living beings. In the animal realm, there are asuras among creatures that fly in the air, those on the land, and those in the water. Crocodiles are an instance of asuras

若詳細分析阿修羅，在這個九法界裏頭的眾生，有五個法界裏頭都有阿修羅。在這個畜生法界裏邊，飛禽有飛禽的阿修羅，走獸有走獸的阿修羅，在水裏的動物有水裏的阿修羅。好像那個鱷魚，那就是水裏的阿修羅。馬也有阿修羅，所謂「害群之馬」，有這個馬在這兒，這一個馬群就不平安了，就很多麻煩，這叫害群之馬。這害群之馬是馬裏頭的阿修羅。這個牛呢？牛也多數是阿修羅，你看那個牛頭上生兩個角，這個角就是表示自己這個硬，能頂其他的東西，用頭來頂，這就是阿修羅的性，說「牛性」，牛性就是阿修羅。狗更是阿修羅！所以你們誰願意養狗的人，就是親近阿修羅；你親近阿修羅，將來和阿修羅就會接近了；接近就會有危險，恐怕就走到阿修羅的道裏頭去。那麼各人要特別注意，小心一點，不要跑到阿修羅裏頭去。

in the water. Wild stallions are asuras among horses. They bring trouble and disturbance to the herd. Most bulls are asuras, too. They butt their two horns against things to show their tough asura disposition. Bulls are asuras by nature. Dogs have even more of an asura nature, so people who own dogs are in close association with asuras. If you hang around asuras, you become closer to them. And getting close to them is dangerous; you might just fall into the realm of asuras. Everyone should pay attention to this and be careful not to run into the realm of asuras!

界法人

含間降焉
和相尊他
道罪升有
人功德豈

The Dharma Realm
of
People

The way of men is harmony,
With merit and
error interspersed.
On virtuous deeds you rise;
offenses make you fall.
It has nothing to do
with anyone else at all.

人道和合，功罪相間；
德升孽降，豈有他焉！

阿修羅道是這樣危險，那麼人道呢？人道也有善，也有惡，所以說「人道和合，功罪相間；德升孽降，豈有他焉！」這個人，性情很溫和的，和誰都能合得來，所以說「人道和合」。

來做人，也不是完全善，也不是完全惡。完全善就升到天上去了，完全惡又去做畜生、做餓鬼、墮地獄了。所以啊！又有一點功，又有一點罪，或者功多過少，或者功少過多。功多罪少的，就生在富貴的家庭；功少罪多的，就生在貧困的家庭。在這裏邊，千差萬別，這種差別性是很多的。

所以說「功罪相間」：有一點功，又有一點過，不是純陰，也不是純陽。純陰的，就是會變鬼去，不會做人了；純陽的，就升天了，不會做人了。所以我們做人，就又可以上天，又可以墮地獄。

「德升孽降」：你做善功德，就向上升一升；你若造

Verse:

The way of men is harmony,
With merit and error interspersed.
On virtuous deeds you rise; offenses make you fall.
It has nothing to do with anyone else at all.

Commentary:

The realm of asuras is dangerous, but what about the realm of people? There are both good and evil people. *The way of men is harmony.* People are harmonious beings who are capable of getting along with anyone.

However, those who become human beings are neither completely good nor completely bad. Beings who are completely good are reborn in the heavens, while those who are thoroughly bad become animals or hungry ghosts or fall into the hells. People have both merit and offenses. When a person's merit is greater than his offenses, he will be born into a rich and distinguished family, but one with small merit and heavy offenses will be born into a poor family. Between these extremes are a thousand differences and a myriad distinctions. Therefore, the verse says: *With merit and error interspersed.* They have some merit, and they also have some offenses; they are neither extremely *yin* nor extremely *yang.* Beings with a preponderance of *yin* become ghosts. Those who are mostly *yang* become gods; they don't become humans.

Human beings can ascend to the heavens or fall into the hells. If

罪孽過，就向下降一降。所以說德升，你造德行，就向上升；你造罪業，就向下降。

「豈有他焉」：其他人不會教你墮地獄，不會教你去做餓鬼，不會教你去變畜生，都是你自己造的。所謂「自作自受」，自己做，自己就去受去。這是人道。

you do good deeds, you ascend; if you commit offenses, you fall. So the verse says: *On virtuous deeds you rise; offenses make you fall.*

It has nothing to do with anyone else at all. Other people cannot tell you to fall into the hells, make you a ghost, or cause you to become an animal. It is entirely up to you. What you create you must endure. You must suffer the consequences of your own actions.

界貪厭白辮
法好無作莫
生生而黑非
畜畜多將是

The Dharma Realm
of
Animals

Eager animals feed on greed,
Never sated by a lot.
They take what's black
  as white
And can't distinguish
  wrong from right.

畜生好貪，多而無厭；
將黑作白，是非莫辨。

前邊所講的七個法界，都是好一點的法界，可以試一試，到那兒去作一作戲去。唯獨現在這三個法界，這不可以嘗試的，不可以去試試看的。你試試看，恐怕就跑不出來了。「一失人身，萬劫不復」，你把這個人身失去了，一萬個大劫恐怕也再得不著人身，所以這是很危險的。不可以好像作戲那麼樣去作一作這個戲。雖然有人說：「好像作戲似的。」但是他還沒有認識這個作戲怎樣做法，他這種無明的見解是見不清楚的，他還認識不清楚。

這畜生不是一類的畜生，畜生也有百千萬億，種類不同，有飛的畜生，有走的畜生，有水裏頭的畜生，有旱陸的畜生，有虛空的畜生。你看這個畜生，單單那飛的畜生，就有百千萬億種不同類的樣子，這飛的眾生有這麼多。那麼走的畜生呢？也不少。小的，老鼠是很小的畜生；大的，這個大笨象是大的畜生。這個鹿、熊、馬、牛，都是很大的畜生。在陸地上的畜生，也有百千萬億種。在水裏的畜生，有水狗、水牛、水馬、海裏頭的豬，也有百千萬億種。

我們人恐怕沒有法子完全都知道；就研究物理、化學

Verse:

Eager animals feed on greed,
Never sated by a lot.
They take what's black as white
And can't distinguish wrong from right.

Commentary:

The seven Dharma Realms discussed above are the better ones. If you wish, you can enter them to try them out—put on a play—but you shouldn't play around with the remaining three Dharma Realms. If you try these out, you may not be able to escape. It is said that once you lose your human form, ten thousand eons may pass before that form can be obtained again. It's very dangerous; you shouldn't treat it as mere play-acting. One of my disciples compared it to putting on a play, but he doesn't really understand what's going on.

There are billions of animals, an infinite variety—flying, crawling, swimming, or walking—in the sky, on land, and in the water. The species of birds and flying animals alone number in the millions, and land animals are not a few, either. There are millions of land animals ranging from small rodents through cows, horses, deer, and bears to the mighty elephant. In the water are seals, water buffalo, sea horses, manatees, and a myriad variety of swimming creatures.

We could never thoroughly study and understand all these animals. Even Ph.D.'s in the areas of zoology, biology, and related

的，研究生物學的、動物學的這一些個人，無論你是個博士，是個什麼士，是個專家，都沒有法子完全知道的。你知道一千種，那一千一百種的，你就不知道了。你知道一千一百種，一千二百種那個，你又不知道了。

那麼你說你完全知道，你怎麼就知道，比你知道的，再沒有更多的呢？這你又不知道了，所以沒有法子完全知道。就這個畜生的種類，我們人就沒有法子知道。爬的畜生，好像就單單蟲類，你都不知道有多少種類。所以這個世間上，你看是不是重重無盡呢？是不是無盡重重呢？

這一些個畜生，都是從什麼地方變的畜生呢？只是從一個字變的畜生——貪！「畜生好貪」：好貪，就是無論什麼，都是多多益善，少少不行。所以說「多而無厭」：因為牠多而不厭，所以「將黑作白」：黑的，牠也不知道是黑的，牠說：「哦！這是白的。」將黑作白，這就表示牠沒有理性了。沒有理性，就是貪多；無論什麼都貪多，甚至於狗屎，牠也貪多。像那狗吃糞，牠愈吃愈多一點，牠就最好了。那麼邋遢的東西，人一看：「哦！那怎麼吃法呢？」牠就愈吃，愈覺得愈香愈甘美，就是這樣子，多而無厭。將黑作

fields who do extensive and continuous research have no way to know all the animal species in the world. If they know a thousand, they don't know eleven hundred. If they know eleven hundred, they don't know twelve hundred.

Although someone might claim to know them all, how can he be certain that someone doesn't know more than he does? It's impossible to be sure. We have no way to completely know all the species of animals. Even the number of different kinds of insects would be hard to determine. When examined like that, wouldn't you say that the world is multilayered and infinite, infinite and multilayered?

Beings become animals as the result of one thing: greed. *Eager animals feed on greed.* For them, no matter what it is, the more the better. A little won't do. They are insatiably greedy; they never get tired of more.

Since they are *never sated by a lot,* they can't tell that black is black. They say, "Oh, it's white!" *They take what's black as white.* Because they are greedy for everything, they have no conceptions we consider reasonable—even to the point that they are greedy to eat excrement. The more excrement a dog eats, the better it likes it. People wonder how it can eat such filth, but the dog finds it more savory with every mouthful. That's how they are—never sated by a lot! That's an example of taking black as white: They delight in something that is basically unpleasant. Greed can extend even to the desire for more sickness. One

白，不好的，牠也認爲好，什麼牠都貪多。甚至於有病，牠也貪多一點病，一個病牠嫌不夠，要兩個病，吃藥牠要吃多一點，這都是貪多。

「是非莫辨」：牠也不知道對，也不知道是不對，是非都不辨了，不清楚了，這就是沒有理性了。怎麼搞的牠沒有個理性呢？就因爲有個「貪」字。有這一個貪字，就糊塗了，就無明蓋覆了；無明把牠蓋住了，什麼牠也不知道。

所以我們人不要貪，不要説：「錢多，出家人不貪財——愈多愈好。」你貪多就有危險。貪多，就容易變畜生，我告訴你！説是：「那我們出家人不會墮落的。」不會墮落？你若不依照佛的戒律去修行，墮落更快一點。所以古來人有那麼一句話，説：「地獄門前僧道多。」都在那等著要到地獄去。那個貪心的老道、貪心的和尚，都在地獄門前等著，説：「快點教我墮地獄囉！快點教我先進去囉！進去很好玩的，在裏邊！」他覺得那個地方是很好玩的地方，所以他要去。去到那兒就知道不是很好玩的地方。

sickness is not enough; they want two. They also want to take more medicine.

And they *can't distinguish wrong from right.* Animals are not clear about right and wrong, because they lack the ability to reason. How did they get that way? Simply through greed. They become muddled, and ignorance envelops them so that they become totally oblivious to anything rational.

Take heed, and don't be greedy. People who have left the home-life should not be greedy for money, but some say "the more the better!" Such greed puts you in grave danger, and it is easy to become an animal as a result.

"People who have left the home-life can't fall," you may say.

If they don't cultivate according to the Buddha's precepts, they will fall even faster. The ancients had a saying, "Many of those standing at the gates of the hells are Sanghans and Taoists." All the old Taoists and Buddhist monks who were greedy are waiting at the doors of hell saying, "Quick! Send me to the hells. Hurry up and let me come in!" Once in, it's a lot of fun inside. They think the hells will provide good entertainment, so they go there. But once they arrive they realize it is not a game.

餓鬼法界

瞋因倒深
喜迷顛月
類果明積
鬼時無日

The Dharma Realm of Hungry Ghosts

*The ghostly crew delights
   in hate,
Deluded by effects,
   confused about cause;
Their ignorance and
   upside-downness
Grow greater each day,
   deeper each month.*

鬼類喜瞋，昧果迷因；
無明顛倒，日積月深。

一般人都知道鬼，有的人就相信有鬼，有的人就說沒有鬼，甚至於佛教徒也不相信有鬼。什麼叫鬼？鬼就是一股陰氣。他有影而無形，有形而無影。你或者看著他一個黑影，你細一研究，他又沒有了。或者看見他好像是個人似的，可是轉眼間也沒有了。這種的道理是很不容易把他弄清楚的。

我們現在所講的是十法界，這十法界之中就有一個鬼法界。這鬼有多少種呢？鬼的種類也像恒河沙數那麼多，無窮無盡，那麼多的種類。有的是有財鬼；怎麼叫有財鬼呢？他就有勢力！在鬼之中，他是做鬼王的。有的無財鬼；無財鬼就是沒有勢力的，也就是窮鬼，因為他窮，所以他就給人很多麻煩，到處去給人添麻煩。那麼你若想明白這鬼的種類有多少，你就要修道，等你開了五眼六通了，那麼有多少種鬼你都會知道了。

有的人說沒有鬼。我就告訴他，若沒有鬼，也就沒有佛，也沒有人，也沒有一切的畜生了。因為畜生也是鬼變的，人也都是鬼變的，阿修羅都是從鬼變的，乃

Verse:

The ghostly crew delights in hate,
Deluded by effects, confused about cause;
Their ignorance and upside-downness
Grow greater each day, deeper each month.

Commentary:

Almost everyone has heard of ghosts, but not everyone believes
in them. There are even Buddhist disciples who don't believe
there are ghosts. Ghosts are masses of *yin* energy that have
shadow and no form, or form and no shadow. Perhaps you have
seen a dark shadow, but when you looked closer it disappeared.
Or perhaps you've seen what seemed like a person, but which
vanished in the blink of an eye. Such phenomena are difficult to
understand.

Among the Ten Dharma Realms, we are now discussing the
Dharma Realm of ghosts. There are as many different kinds of
ghosts as there are grains of sand in the Ganges River. There are
infinitely many kinds of ghosts. Some are affluent and powerful
ghosts that reign as kings over the ghosts' realm. Some ghosts are
poverty-stricken and devoid of authority—it is often the poor
ghosts who bother people and go about causing trouble. If you
want to know how many kinds of ghosts there are, work hard at
cultivation, open the five eyes and six spiritual penetrations, and
then you'll know.

As to people who say there are no ghosts, I tell them that if there
are no ghosts, then there are also no Buddhas, people, or animals,

至於天道、阿羅漢、緣覺、菩薩、佛，都是從鬼道上來的。因爲什麼呢？因爲這「十法界不離一念心」。這一念心，就造成十法界。

你做鬼事，就是墮落鬼道去；做人事，就到人道裏頭去；做阿修羅的事，就跑到阿修羅裏頭去。你做阿羅漢的事，就跑到阿羅漢裏邊去；你做緣覺，就跑到緣覺裏邊去；你若做菩薩的事，就跑到菩薩的眷屬裏邊去；你若做佛事，就成佛；你若做地獄的事，就墮地獄。這都是由你現前的一念心造成的，所以才說十法界不出這個一念。

那麼現在講這個鬼，「鬼類喜瞋」：凡是鬼的種類，就歡喜發火，生瞋恨心。人家對他好，他也生瞋恨心；對他不好，他也生個瞋恨心。他最歡喜是什麼呢？就是給其他的人麻煩。你對他好，他也給你麻煩；你對他不好，他也給你麻煩。所以就說，燒香引出鬼來了。本來你燒香，是恭敬他。你不恭敬他，他還不給你麻煩；你一恭敬他，他就給你麻煩，讓你生病了。所以孔子都講：「敬鬼神而遠之。」這鬼神，你恭敬是要恭敬，但是你不要和他接近，要離他這一點，所以說鬼類喜瞋。

because animals are transformed from ghosts, as are people, asuras, and so forth, even to gods, Arhats, Pratyekabuddhas, Bodhisattvas, and Buddhas. All realms come from the realm of ghosts, because the Ten Dharma Realms are not apart from a single thought of the mind, and one thought of the mind creates the Ten Dharma Realms.

By conducting yourself as if you were a ghost, you fall into the ghosts' realm. Acting as a person does, you come to the human realm. Behaving like an asura, you join the ranks of asuras. Assuming the practice of an Arhat, you enter the realm of Arhats. Behaving like One Enlightened to Conditions, you enter that realm. Doing the deeds of a Bodhisattva, you join the retinue of Bodhisattvas. Performing the work of a Buddha, you realize Buddhahood. If you commit hellish offenses, you fall into the hells. All of this is brought about by the one thought that is right now in your mind. Thus we say that the Ten Dharma Realms are not beyond a single thought.

The ghostly crew delights in hate. Ghosts enjoy exploding in a fiery rage when people are not good to them, and even when treated well they still get angry. They like nothing better than giving people trouble. They give you trouble whether you are good to them or not. There is an old saying: "Lighting a stick of incense calls forth ghosts." People light incense to pay respect to ghosts. Before you've paid respect to them they don't bother you, but once you make their acquaintance, the ghosts become a nuisance, make you sick, or give you some other trouble. Confucius said, "Respect the ghosts and spirits, but keep them at a distance." It is

「昧果迷因」：果，他也不明白；因，他也不懂，迷昧因果了，所以他就不知道好壞。本來種好因結好果，種善因結善果，種不善因就結惡果；種瓜就得瓜，種豆就得豆。他不懂這個，他不懂什麼叫種瓜得瓜，什麼叫種豆得豆。他就種上茄子，想要吃辣椒；種上辣椒，他就想吃黃瓜。所以他就不懂這個道理，就是「亂晒囉」（廣東俗語），就是亂七八糟的這麼胡搞，這叫昧果迷因，不懂因果的。

他的「無明顛倒」，這種行爲「日積月深」：日積，就一天一天地積得很多；月深，這無明顛倒，這個月比那個月深一點，那個月又比那個月深一點。就是愈造愈深，愈深他愈造。所以講日積月深。

wise to pay respect to the ghosts and spirits, but otherwise keep your distance and don't get too close to them.

Deluded by effects, confused about cause. They are unclear about results and don't understand their causes. As a result, they can't tell good from bad. Basically if you plant a good cause, you reap a good fruit; if you plant a bad cause you reap a bad effect. If you plant melons you get melons; plant beans and you'll get beans. Ghosts don't understand that. They plant eggplant and anticipate eating hot peppers, or plant hot peppers and think they will harvest cucumbers. Since they have no comprehension of principles, they act recklessly and in confusion.

Their ignorance and upside-downness / Grow greater each day, deeper each month. They accumulate a lot karma every day. Their ignorance and upside-downness become deeper with each passing month. The more karma they create, the deeper their ignorance gets, and the deeper it gets, the more offenses they commit.

地獄法界

地獄無起受　獄門惑報　憂自造循　苦鑽業環

The Dharma Realm
of
Hell-beings

*The hells' anxiety and
suffering
Is devoid of doors,
    yet one bores right in.
Giving rise to delusion,
    deeds are done.
The retribution is borne
    in due accord.*

地獄憂苦，無門自鑽；
起惑造業，受報循環。

還剩一個法界，「地獄憂苦，無門自鑽；起惑造業，受報循環。」

「地獄憂苦」：地獄是最不快樂的一個地方，那麼你們誰願意到那個地方旅行去，隨時都可以到的。誰願意到地獄旅行去，我可以保證你們即刻就到。怎麼樣子呢？你「愁一愁，就地獄遊一遊。」愁，就是憂愁；你一憂愁，就到地獄旅行去了，vacation（度假）去了。

> 愁一愁，就地獄遊一遊；
> 笑一笑，就老還少；
> 哭一哭，就地獄有個小黑屋。

你看，就這樣子。你要是憂愁，就種地獄的因。你要是笑，就種天堂的因，「自古神仙無別法」，沒有旁的方法，「只生歡喜不生愁」。所以說你「愁一愁，就地獄遊一遊」，到地獄去旅行去了。你能常常地笑，老了也像年輕人一樣。哭這也是一個麻煩的事情。

總而言之，地獄沒有快樂的，地獄就是憂苦的。但是地獄沒有門，地獄這個門是自己開的，自己開這個地

Verse:

The hells' anxiety and suffering
Is devoid of doors, yet one bores right in.
Giving rise to delusion, deeds are done.
The retribution is borne in due accord.

Commentary:

The hells are a miserable place. Anyone who would like to take a vacation in the hells can do so any time at all. I can guarantee that you'll get there right away. How?

It is said,

> *Depressed and melancholy, you roam through the hells.*
> *Happy and smiling, you enjoy eternal youth.*
> *Weeping and woe make a small dark room in the hells.*

Once you become worried, you travel to the hells to take a vacation. If you get worried, you plant a seed for the hells. If you smile, you plant a seed for the heavens. It is said,

> *From ancient times, the divine immortals*
> *have had no other practice*
> *Than merely being happy and not being sad.*

If you become depressed, you take a trip to the hells. If you smile all the time, you look youthful even if you are old. If you cry, you give yourself a lot of vexation.

獄門，自己就往裏鑽，鑽到裏邊去，所以說「無門自鑽」：本來地獄沒有門，不像我們人間的監獄，用人工造成了，放在那地方，誰犯法了，把他放到監獄去。不是的！地獄沒有門，但是你到了自己應該入地獄時，你到那兒，那個門就開了。你就硬往裏鑽，鑽不進去也要鑽；無門自鑽。

「起惑造業」：爲什麼到地獄去啊？因爲無明、煩惱，你愚癡了、不明白了。因爲不明白了，所以就造出一些個惡業來了。沒有造善業，造惡業。「受報循環」：你造了一些惡業，就要墮地獄，就要受這個果報。受果報是循環無端的。你造什麼業，就受什麼果報，絲毫都不會錯的。所以這叫受報循環。

In general, there is no happiness in the hells. They are full of suffering and distress. *The hells' anxiety and suffering / Is devoid of doors, yet one bores right in.* Unlike jails built to hold criminals, the hells haven't any doors. However, if you are due to go to hell, when you arrive it is just as if a door opened, because you find yourself worming and boring in where there was no entrance.

Giving rise to delusion, deeds are done. Why do you go to the hells? Ignorance and afflictions make you stupid and confused, so you create bad karma and don't do good deeds. *The retribution is borne in due accord.* When you create bad karma, you fall into the hells to undergo the retribution. There is no end to this cycle once it starts. You receive exact repayment for whatever karma you create, and the retribution is never off by even a hair's breadth.

心念念岸
一當此彼
界一當此彼
不離覺登
十不能立

All of tehese tn realms—
a single thought—
Are not apart
from your present thought.
If you can awaken
to that thought,
You'll arrive immediately
at the other shore.

十界一心，不離當念；
能覺此念，立登彼岸。

這十法界，佛、菩薩、聲聞、緣覺，這是四聖法界；
天、人、阿修羅、地獄、餓鬼、畜生，這是六凡法界
。合起來叫十法界。這十法界從什麼地方生出來的？
就從我們人現前這一念心生出來的。所以說「十界一
心，不離當念」：這十法界都沒有離開你，就是現前
這一念。

你現前這一念，你若明白了，所以說「能覺此念」：
你若明白這一念，「立登彼岸」：立刻就到彼岸了，
這個彼岸是什麼呢？就是覺悟。覺悟就是不迷惑了，
就把無明破了。破無明，那個法身就現出來了，所以
說立登彼岸，立刻就到彼岸了，就「摩訶般若波羅蜜
」了。

Verse:

All of these ten realms—a single thought—
Are not apart from your present thought.
If you can awaken to that thought,
You'll arrive immediately at the other shore.

Commentary:

Buddhas, Bodhisattvas, Hearers, and Those Enlightened to Conditions are the Four Sagely Dharma Realms; gods, human beings, asuras, hell-beings, hungry ghosts, and animals are the Six Common Dharma Realms. Together, they make up the Ten Dharma Realms. Where do the Ten Dharma Realms come from? From the single thought which is right now in your mind. *All of these ten realms—a single thought— / Are not apart from your present thought.*

If you can awaken to that thought, if you can understand it, *you'll arrive immediately at the other shore.* The other shore is enlightenment. When you become enlightened, you are no longer confused. When ignorance is smashed and the Dharma-body appears, you arrive at the other shore. This is Mahapraja-paramita.

如意魔女

我今天晚間想起這個如意女來了。她是周朝的一個鬼，被雷劈了；她又修成一種魔術，雷也沒有法子打她了。那麼她就各處去作怪，然後就遇到我了，她要皈依三寶，現在是改邪歸正了。這要是說起來啊，可以寫一本書。現在你們不要怕她了；她即使來到這地方，也不會害人了。

在二十七年以前，大約是在中華民國三十四年（西元一九四五年）二月十二這一天，我在東北周家棧這個地方，有一個「道德會」。道德會，就是講道德的地方，天天都講演。這個會上有我幾個皈依弟子，所以每逢從那兒經過的時候，我就到那地方住幾天。

住幾天就遇到一個不知姓什麼的批八字的先生。怎麼叫批八字呢？就是你年上兩個字，月上有兩個字，日上有兩個字，時上又有兩個字。他給人批八字批得很靈的，他就給我批，他說：「喔！你啊！應該去作官去，怎麼來出家了呢？你若作官，會作很大的官。」我說：「官怎麼樣作呢？我都不會，也不知道怎麼樣作官，怎麼可以作呢？我會作和尚，所以我現在出家

The As-You-Wish Demon Woman

I've suddenly thought of the story of the "As-You-Wish Woman." She was a ghost that had been shattered by thunder in the Zhou Dynasty. She then practiced a kind of magic that protected her from thunder, and when she mastered it, she went around causing trouble. Later she met me, took refuge with the Triple Jewel, and reformed herself. I could write an entire book on this. You don't have to be afraid of her; even if she were to come here, she wouldn't harm anyone.

Twenty-seven years ago [1945], on the twelfth day of the second month, I passed through the Zhou family station in Manchuria. In the town there was a Virtue Society whose members met daily for lectures on morality. Since some of the members were my disciples, I would usually stay in the town for a few days when I passed through.

This time I met a Chinese astrologer who cast people's horoscopes by looking at the eight characters (two for the year, two for the month, two for the day, and two for the hour) of their birth. His horoscopes were very efficacious. He cast my horoscope and said, "You should be an official. Why have you left home? Had you wanted to, you could have been a great official."

113

。」他說這個太可惜了。這是在周家棧,這個批命的他這麼給我批。然後又看我的手,他說:「噢!你這個手,最低限度,你可以中一個頭名狀元。」

我就說:「現在我連最後那一名都中不了了,還中頭名?」然後他又細看說:「哦,你啊!今年是走運了!今年你有吉祥的事情!」

我說:「有什麼吉祥的事情呢?」他說:「過下個月初十,你就和現在不同了。」

我說:「怎麼樣不同法呢?」他說:「以前一千里地以內的人相信你,過了初十之後,一萬里地以內的人就都相信你了。」

我說:「這個怎麼會這樣子呢?」他說:「到時候你就知道了!」那麼說完了這話,我又住了兩天。大約是二月十四、十五的樣子,我就到那個鑲白旗四屯。鑲白旗四屯有我的皈依弟子,叫夏遵祥,他那年已經六十多歲了。他家裏有三十多口人,種了很多地,可以說是個財主。在那一個鄉下,他是最有錢的。那麼這個老人從來也不相信佛,什麼都不相信,等見著我來了,他就相信,要皈依。不單他一個人要皈依,全家都要皈依,所以他全家就都皈依我了。以後我每逢到那個地方去,就到他家裏去住。他家裏三十多口人

"I haven't any idea how to be an official," I said. "But I do know how to be a Buddhist monk, and so I have left home."

"What a pity," said the astrologer, and he looked at my hands. "At the very least," he said, "you could have been a top-ranking imperial scholar."

"No," I said. "I couldn't even have come in last."

He looked my hands again and said, "Oh, this year something very lucky will happen to change your life!"

"What could that be?" I asked.

"After the tenth of the next month you will be different from now," he replied.

"Different in what way?"

"Right now, all the people within 1000 *li* [350 miles] believe in you, but after the tenth of next month, everyone within 10,000 *li* [3500 miles] will believe in you."

"How can that be?" I asked.

，我一去，都高興得不得了。在那住了大約有十天的樣子，就又有七、八十人都皈依，大約是七十二個人也都來皈依。

皈依之後，等到二十五這天，我就坐著夏遵祥他家裏的車到雙城縣去，他家裏離雙城縣有七十多里路。這車要一早晨三點多鐘就開始走。

這時候雖然說三月間，正是冷的時候，冷得不得了。這個趕車的人和跟車的人都要穿著皮衣、皮襖、皮褲，戴著皮帽子。我呢，那時候是很窮的，穿的衣服就三層布，這一個衲袍是三層布，穿的褲子也是兩層布的褲子——夾褲；穿鞋是穿鞋，沒有穿襪子。就穿羅漢鞋，有窟窿的那種鞋，沒有穿襪子。一早這車就走了，我坐在車上邊。我戴著個帽子，也遮不住耳朵，那是一個合掌巾，那種帽子就好像人合著掌那個樣子的。你們看見濟公戴的那個帽子，就那個樣子的。

坐在車上，七十里路，從三點鐘大約坐到一早七點鐘吧。到了城裏了，天也光了。這趕車的老闆和跟著車的人呢，心裏想一定會把我凍死在車上，因為穿的衣服也少，又在這車上。他們都坐坐車，下來跑一跑，因為不跑就凍得不得了，一定要下來活動活動。我在車上，由一出門口，就坐在車上。到雙城縣的東門外，把車停住了。我從車上下來，這個趕車的一看，「

"When the time comes, you will know," he said.

Two days later, on the fourteenth or fifteenth of the second month, I went to the village of Xiangbaichi, fourth district, and stayed with my disciple Xia Zunxiang, who was over sixty years old and had a family of over thirty people. He was one of the richest landowners in the area and had never believed in Buddhism or anything else. But when he saw me, he believed in me and wanted to take refuge with me. He and his whole family took refuge, and every time I went to the village I'd stay at his house. His family of over thirty was extremely happy to see me this time. I stayed with them for ten days, and about seventy-two people came to take refuge.

On the twenty-fifth, I set out in Mr. Xia's cart for Shuangcheng County. Since it was over seventy *li* [25 miles] away, we left at three o'clock in the morning.

Although it was early spring, the weather was bitter cold. The driver and the attendant were dressed in fur coats, trousers, and hats. Being very poor, I wore only my usual rag robe made of three layers of thin cotton cloth, trousers made of two layers of cloth, open Arhat sandals with no socks, and a hat shaped like folded palms that didn't cover my ears. That was the kind of hat that Master Ji Gong wore.

We rode from three in the morning until dawn, reaching the city at seven in the morning. The driver and the attendant thought I would

117

哦！還沒有凍死他！」他以為我一定會凍死。

二十五這天我到雙城縣。有一些個善友，有一些個護法居士，我到他們家裏去，也住了十多天。等三月初九又回到鑲白旗四屯，回到夏遵祥的家裏。他就告訴我了，他說有一個夏文山，他有一個女兒，就是在我打皈依的時候一起皈依的，她最近有病了，病得很厲害，六、七天不吃東西、不喝水，也不講話，就很大的脾氣，發脾氣要打人的樣子。等到初九這一天，她的母親就來對我講，說：「師父啊！我這個女兒啊，皈依之後沒過幾天，她就病了。病得很厲害，她也不講話，也不吃東西，也不喝水，天天都瞪著眼睛，把頭栽到炕上，也不講話，不知道她這是個什麼病？」

當時我就對她講，我說：「我也不會給人治病，她什麼病，你問我是不行的。現在我有皈依弟子叫韓崗吉，他是開五眼的，能知道人的過去未來，前生是怎麼回事，他也知道；你今生什麼事情，他也知道。你問他去。」那麼她就問這個韓崗吉。

這韓崗吉也是在我到雙城縣，二十五號以前的時候他皈依的。他皈依的時候，本來我不收他。為什麼不收他呢？因為在我沒出家以前，他和我是很好的朋友，在道德會上是同事。因為他開眼了，我出家之後，他

freeze to death, since I was so insufficiently dressed. They had stopped reeep warm, but I had remained in the cart from the beginning of the trip. When we arrived at the eastern gate of Shuangcheng County and I got out of the cart, the driver exclaimed, "Oh, we thought surely you had frozen to death!"

I stayed with friends, Dharma protecting laymen, for more than ten days, and on the ninth of the third month, I returned to Xia Zunxiang's home in Xiangbaichi. When I arrived, he told me that one of my recent disciples, the daughter of Xia Wenshan, had fallen dangerously ill. She hadn't eaten or drunk water for six or seven days. She did not speak, and she looked fiercely angry, as if she wanted to beat people.

Then her mother came. "Master," she said, "my daughter became very ill a few days after taking refuge. She won't talk, eat, or drink, but just glares and sticks her head on the bed. I don't know what illness she has."

I said to her, "I can't cure her, so it's useless to ask me. However, my disciple Han Gangji has opened his five eyes and knows people's past, present, and future affairs. You should ask him."

Han Gangji had also taken refuge on the twenty-fourth of the second month. At first I had refused to take him as a disciple, because before I had left home, the two of us had been good friends and had worked together in the Virtue Society. After I left

見到我，他開眼一看，他說：「原來你生生世世都是我的師父來著！」所以就要皈依我。

我說：「我不能收你做徒弟，我們本來都是老朋友來著，我怎麼可以收你做徒弟呢？」他說：「不是，我自己現在知道我自己……。」他說如果我不收他皈依，這一生他就要墮落了。說這話之後，他就跪在地上不起來，一定要皈依。我就一定不收他。

經過大約有半點多鐘，時間不太長。我就問他，我說：「皈依我的人，都要依教奉行。你現在這麼大的本事，又知道過去，又知道未來，又知道現在，那麼你知道是知道，你會不會有一種貢高的心，不聽師父的教訓？」他說他一定會聽的：「師父！您教我赴湯我就赴湯，教我蹈火就蹈火。赴湯蹈火，在所不辭！」就是到了滾水裏頭去，那有一鍋滾水，師父您教我去，我就跳到那滾水裏去，煮熟了也不要緊，這叫赴湯。蹈火，那有一堆火，您教我到那火上走，我也要去的。

我說：「真的？可是真的啊？你不能將來我有事情教你做的時候，你不幹啊！」他說：「無論什麼事情，師父您教我做，我一定做的，就算有什麼危險我也不怕的。」那好啦，於是乎在這七十二個人裏頭，他也就皈依了。

home and Han Gangji opened his five eyes, he saw that, life after life, I had always been his teacher. And so he wanted to take refuge with me.

I said, "We're good friends; how could I take you as a disciple?"

"But if I don't take refuge with you, I shall certainly fall in this life," Han Gangji said, and he knelt on the ground and refused to get up.

I was just as determined not to accept him, but after perhaps half an hour, I finally said, "Those who take refuge with me must follow instructions. You have talent; you know the past, present, and future. Is it possible that it has caused you to become arrogant? Will your pride prevent you from obeying my instructions?"

"Master," he said, "I'll certainly obey. If you tell me to throw myself into a cauldron of boiling water, I'll do it. If you tell me to walk on fire, I'll walk. If I get boiled or burned to death, that's all right."

"You'd better be telling the truth," I said. "If I give you instructions, you can't ignore them."

"No matter what it is," he said, "if you tell me to do it, I will do it, and fear no danger whatsoever."

那麼這一次我就叫他，我說：「你能給人家看病，現在我這皈依弟子有病了，你給看一看啦！」他就坐那兒一打坐，這麼一觀想，這要作觀想的，這一觀想，哦！看他面啊，就嚇得那個樣子，不得了了，就害怕了，告訴我：「師父！這個事情不能管的！這個事情啊，我無論如何管不了的！」我說：「怎麼樣子？」

他說：「這個是一個魔啊！這個魔啊，可太厲害了，她能變化人形，啊！能變成人形，在這個世界搗亂害人，這個魔才厲害呢！」我說：「怎麼那麼厲害？你說一說看。」

他說這個魔是周朝的一個魔。周朝那時候她是一個鬼，因爲她不守規矩，就被一個有道行、有神通的人，用雷把她劈碎了。但是她這個靈性還沒有完全散，所以以後她又聚回到一起了，又變成一個魔。現在這個魔，她的神通特別大；她能飛行變化，忽然就沒有了，忽然又有了。

他說她因爲被雷劈過，所以以後啊，她就又修成了，她煉一種法寶，這種法寶呢，是專門避雷的。這法寶是什麼煉的呢？就是那個女人生小孩子，小孩子初初生出來外邊的那層皮，那層包小孩子的皮。她用那層皮修煉，煉成一個帽子，這麼一個黑帽子。她把這個

And so Han Gangji was one of the seventy-two people who took refuge on the twenty-fourth.

Hearing that one of my disciples was sick, I told Han Gangji, "You can diagnose illnesses. Take a look."

Han Gangji sat in meditation and made a contemplative examination of the illness. Suddenly his face blanched with terror. "Master," he said, "we can't handle this one. It's beyond our control."

"What is it?" I asked.

"The demon who is causing the illness is extremely violent and can assume human form to bring chaos into the world and injury to humankind."

"What makes the demon so fierce?" I asked.

"The demon was a ghost long ago in the Zhou Dynasty," he said. "Because it didn't behave properly, a virtuous man with spiritual powers shattered it with thunder. But the ghost's spirit did not completely disperse, and it later fused into a powerful demon that could fly and vanish and appear again, at will."

"The demon has refined a magic weapon," he continued. "It's an

帽子戴到頭上，什麼雷也打不了她了，雷因爲怕污穢
的東西。

西方人認爲雷是沒有人來支配的。普通的雷可能是沒
有人支配，但是有一種特別的雷，就是有一種神，用
雷來懲罰世間的妖魔鬼怪的。她煉成這個帽子，這個
雷就劈不了她了。她又煉成兩個法寶，就是兩個圓圓
的球。她用這個帽子，若給人戴上她這帽子，這個人
哪，靈魂就會被她捉去了，就變成她的眷屬了。那麼
她這個球，如果打在人身上，人就會死了。就這麼厲
害。

所以這韓崗吉看出來，她是這麼厲害的一個魔鬼，就
告訴我，説：「師父啊！這事情不能管的！」我説：
「那不能管，這有病的怎麼辦呢？」他説：「這個有
病的，那一定死的！沒有辦法的！」

我説：「死？怎麼可以的！她若是沒有皈依我，當然
我不管。她上個月二十四號皈依我的，還沒有那麼久
。」當時皈依我的時候，我就教那一班人念〈大悲咒
〉。我説：「你們每一個人都應該學〈大悲咒〉，將
來會有用的。遇到什麼危急的時候，你念〈大悲咒〉
，觀音菩薩就會保護著你。」於是乎，他們就有很多
人念〈大悲咒〉。

exclusive anti-thunder device: a black hat made out of the thin membranes that cover the bodies of newborn children. When she wears the hat, the thunder cannot hurt her, because thunder has a great aversion to filth."

Westerners think that thunder has no one controlling it, and while that may be the case for ordinary thunder, there is a special kind of thunder that is used by gods to punish the goblins, demons, and ghosts who wander throughout the world.

In addition to the black hat, which protected her from thunder, she had refined two other magic weapons: two round balls. If she put her hat on someone, his soul would fall under her control, and he would become one of her followers. If she hit someone with one of the two round balls, he would immediately die.

Han Gangji saw that she was such a fierce demon and said, "Master, we can't handle this one."

"Then what will become of the sick girl?" I asked.

"She will certainly die; there's no way to help her," he said.

"I can't allow her to die. If she weren't my disciple I'd pay no attention, but she took refuge with me on the twenty-fourth of last month."

我説：「她若不皈依我，那麼這個魔鬼抓她去、不抓她去，我不管。現在已經皈依我了，我就不許可這魔鬼抓她去，教她死。我一定要去管這個事。」他説：「師父啊！那您要去管，我不能去的！我不能跟您去的！」

我説：「什麼？你皈依的時候，你説『赴湯蹈火，在所不辭』，現在還不一定是湯，不一定是火呢？你爲什麼就辭了呢？」他也沒有話講了。沒有話講，想一想就説：「師父！那您要派幾個護法保護著我。」我説：「你不要囉嗦了！跟著走就是了。你囉嗦什麼呢？」那麼他聽我這樣講，也不敢囉嗦了，就跟著我去了。去到那地方，這個有病的人，頭衝著床下，栽到這枕頭上，屁股就撅起來這麼樣子，很難看的。但是很大脾氣，眼睛瞪著有牛眼睛那麼大，尤其看見我，更不高興。

我就問他們家裏，有病的原因。他説，在前七、八天，在他們這條屯的外邊，有一個孤墳。就有一個老太婆，大約有五十多歲，穿著雨藍色的衣服、長衫，頭上梳兩個小辮辮。這個辮子不是向後邊梳的，她的辮是向前邊這麼樣梳的。那麼穿著黃褲子、黃鞋，就在這孤墳哭。

When those people had taken refuge, I had taught them to recite the Great Compassion Mantra. I had said to them, "Each of you should learn to recite the Great Compassion Mantra. It will be of great help to you. If you are in danger and distress and you recite it, Guanyin Bodhisattva will protect you." Since then, many of them had been reciting the Great Compassion Mantra.

I said, "If she hadn't taken refuge with me, I wouldn't care whether the demon took her life or not. But she took refuge with me, so I can't allow the demon to take her life. I've got to do something."

"You take care of it, then," said Han Gangji, "but I'm not going."

"What?" I said, "When you took refuge, you promised me that you would jump into boiling water or walk on fire if I asked you to. Now it's not even boiling water or fire; why have you decided to back out?"

Han Gangji had nothing to say. He thought it over. "If you appoint some Dharma-protecting gods to take care of me..."

"Don't shilly-shally!" I said. "If you're going to go, go. But don't vacillate!"

當時就有一個姓夏的，也是一個老太婆，就去勸她說
：「妳不要哭啦！」她哭什麼呢？這姓夏的老太婆就
聽她說：「我那個人哪？我那個人哪？」就這麼哭，
一邊哭一邊要找她那個人。那麼這個老太婆勸勸她，
她就不哭了，就跟著她，兩個一起到鑲白旗四屯這個
屯裏邊來。兩個人走到這屯的外邊，大約這門口有門
神，她就不敢進來。那條屯有圍牆，四邊都有fence（
圍牆），有四個門，到門外邊她就不敢進來。姓夏這
個女人就自己到這個屯裏來了，她就在這條屯外邊又
在這兒哭。

這時候，夏遵祥他家裏的馬車從外邊回來了。這馬一
看見這個東西就認識！人不認識這個東西，馬認識。
馬一見到這個東西，就驚起來跑了。她就藉著這個車
往門裏頭跑的時候，跟著就進來了。大約那守門的神
在那兒也慌上來了，一看這馬驚了，就不管這門了。
她就跑進來了。

跑進來，就到一個姓尤的家裏。這姓尤的叫尤忠寶。
到他家裏，也是找她那個人。那麼她望望這個姓尤的
，然後從他家裏就出來了。出來這時候，就有三、四
十人圍著這老太婆了，都叫她「老傻太太」。問她：
「姓什麼？」她說：「我也沒有姓」。問她：「叫什
麼名字？」她也沒有名。

He said no more and followed me. When we arrived, the girl was lying on the bed with her head on the pillow and her bottom sticking up in the air; it was an embarrassing sight. Her eyes were as wide as those of a cow, and she glared with rage at me.

I asked the girl's family, "What is the cause of the illness?"

They told me that seven or eight days earlier, an old woman, around age fifty, had been sitting beside an isolated grave outside the village. She was wearing a dark blue gown and had braided her hair backwards in two plaits that went up her head in back and hung down across her temples. She was wearing yellow trousers and shoes, and she was crying mournfully beside the grave. Hearing her cries, the elderly Mrs. Xia went to comfort her, but she continued to cry, "Oh my person, oh my person..." and kept looking for her "person."

Finally she stopped crying, and the two of them walked to the village gate. There must have been a spirit guarding the gate, because the old woman wouldn't go in. The village was surrounded by a wall and had a gate on each of the four sides. Mrs. Xia went in, but the old woman stayed outside the gate, crying.

At that moment Xia Zunxiang's horse cart returned to the village. When it reached the gate the horse saw the woman and shied in

再問她，她說：「我是個死人。」這樣子呢，就有三、四十人圍著她就看。看這個好像一個怪物，這麼看她。她手裏拎著這個黑帽子這麼走。一邊走，好像一個什麼也不懂的人，走到夏文山家後邊的牆，那牆大約有八尺多高，她到牆後邊，把她這個黑帽子一撇，就撇過那個牆裏邊去了。她隨著一跳，啊！八尺多高的牆，她也跳進去了。任何人都跳不進去的牆，她跳進去了。看的這一班人說：「啊！這老傻太太會武術，會功夫！」於是乎，這一班人就跑到前邊門裏邊去看。

夏文山的兒子叫夏遵全，他也是我的皈依弟子，也是皈依沒有兩個禮拜，是二十四日皈依這一班人。從門口進來就說：「媽！媽！媽！老傻太太到我們家裏來了！您不要害怕！」他媽媽巴著脖子盡向外看，也沒有什麼。一回頭，哦，有一個老太婆已經到炕邊上了，要上炕，身體爬到炕上一半，在下邊還有一半，就這麼樣子。這時候她說：「妳找誰啊？妳找誰啊？」她也不說話。那麼過後，她們看見她很奇怪的樣子，這有病的女孩和她媽媽兩個人就念上〈大悲咒〉了，就念「南無喝囉怛那哆囉夜耶……」，這麼一念，她就慢慢、慢慢下地了。這老傻太太下地就躺到炕沿底下，像死人一樣也不動彈了。她們一看，這不得了，這若死在家裏，出人命啦！於是乎她就報告村長。村

fright, for horses can recognize things that people cannot see. As the horse cart went careening through the gate, the old woman followed it in. Probably the spirit who guarded the gate had his back turned, and in the confusion, she went sneaking through.

The old woman ran to the house of Mr. Yu Zhongbao and continued to look for her "person." She looked at Mr. Yu and then ran out of the house, where she was surrounded by thirty or forty curious onlookers who jeered at her, "Stupid old woman! What's your last name?"

"I don't have a last name."

"What's your first name?" they asked.

"I don't know. I'm a corpse," she said. They looked at her as if she were a freak. She continued to walk as if in a stupor until she reached the back wall of Xia Wenshan's estate. She then threw her hat over the eight-foot wall, and in one jump, leapt right over after it. No one else could have jumped over the wall, but she made it.

"The stupid old woman knows kung fu!" the crowd screeched, and they ran around and went in through the front gate to watch her.

Xia Wenshan's son Xia Zunquan, who had also taken refuge on

長來了，看見有這麼一個老年的女人躺在地下，好像要死的樣子，於是乎，這個村長就伸手，用一隻手就把這個老女人拿起來了，就拿到外面去，放在地下，教她這麼走。等她走到鄉公所裏邊去，就問她：「妳是哪裏人呀？妳幹什麼來的？」

她就對著這些個人說她是死人，說：「你不要問我，我就是死人，我也沒有姓，也沒有名，也沒有住的地方。我到什麼地方，就住在什麼地方。」這個村長聽她這麼講，看她這個樣子，也都很驚恐了。於是乎帶著槍就把她向屯外邊送，向西邊送。

頭一次，送了五十幾步遠，這個人回來了，人回來，等到向屯的門口回頭一望，這老女人還跟在後邊。於是乎就又向遠的處送她。這一回就送出七十幾步遠，那麼這個人又回來了，走到半路上，這個老女人又跟著回來了。這一次，和他一同有三、四個鄉屯裏頭的人，就又往遠的處送她。這回送出一百五十多步遠，就教她趕快走，不走就用槍打她。那麼這個村長，就在那兒放了兩槍，這個老女人就趴在地下。本來不是打她，但是她嚇得就趴在地上，大約她以為又是打雷了。這回村長回來一看，沒有跟著回來。於是這村長和鄉公所裏幾個辦事的人員，就回到屯裏頭了。

這個老的女人雖然走了，可是夏文山的家裏，他的女

the twenty-fourth, ran in the door. "Mama! Mama! The stupid old woman is in our house, but don't be afraid."

His mother looked out the window, but saw nothing strange. When she turned around, there was the old woman crawling up on the brick bed. She was halfway on the bed and halfway on the floor.

"What do you want?" shouted the mother, but the old woman made no reply.

Seeing the old woman's strange behavior, the mother and her daughter began immediately to recite the mantra. Just as they recited the first line of the mantra, *Na mo he la da nuo duo la ye ye*, the old woman slipped to the ground and lay inert, exactly like a corpse.

Seeing that, the family was greatly upset. If somebody were to die in their home, it would not be good.

They went for the sheriff. When the sheriff saw the old woman lying on the floor as if she were dying, he picked her up with one hand and set her outside. Then he took her to the village courthouse for questioning. "Where are you from?" he asked, "and why have you come here?"

兒就病了。就是瞪著眼睛，也不說話，也不吃東西，晚間也不睡覺，頭就好像在床上叩頭那麼樣子。就是我前邊說的她這個頭栽在枕頭上，後邊這個身就高起來這麼樣子，七、八天也不吃東西。

我沒有到他家裏以前，我和韓崗吉說：「你說一管這閒事，就會死的，我現在就寧可我自己死，我也要救我這皈依弟子。第一個條件，我要救我自己的皈依弟子，因為她皈依我，我不能看著她死了不管。第二個條件，我要救這個魔。你說這個魔啊，誰也管不了她，但是她造罪造得多了，一定還是會有人管得了她。她修煉了這麼多年，如果有人來把她消滅了，這也是很可惜的。所以第二個條件，我要救這個魔，她就是有本領令我死了，我都要去救她去。第三個條件，我要救世界所有的一切眾生，如果我現在不把她收伏了，將來世界人受害的一定是很多。我有這三個條件，我一定要去。」所以就到這有病的家裏了。

當時這個村長也來了，聽我們一談論起來，一個禮拜以前來的這個老傻太太就是個魔鬼，他也就想起來了，他說：「哦！難怪那天她在地上躺著，我用一隻手把她拿起來，一點都不費力，好像沒有東西似的。若不說我也想不起來，現在一講起來，知道這的確是個魔鬼了。」

"Don't ask me," she said. "I'm a corpse. I have no name and no home. I just live wherever I am."

Frightened by her strange talk and behavior, the sheriff escorted her at pistol point some fifty paces outside the village. But when he returned to the village gate, she was right behind him. He took her seventy paces, and she followed him back again. Finally, he and three deputies took her 150 paces outside the village and said, "Get out or get shot!" and they fired two shots in the air.

The old woman fell to the ground in terror, thinking the shots were thunder, which had destroyed her before. This time she didn't follow them back to the village.

When the sheriff and his men returned, they heard that Xia Wenshan's daughter was sick—not speaking, eating, or sleeping, but just lying on the bed staring in rage with her head on the pillow and her bottom sticking up in the air. She didn't eat for seven or eight days.

Before we went to Xia Wenshan's home, I said to Han Gangji, "You said that if we tried to handle the matter we would die. Well, I would rather die than not save one of my disciples. First of all, I must save those who have taken refuge with me; I can't just stand by and let them die. Secondly, I must save the demon. You say no

135

這樣子呢，我們就要把這個魔鬼又找來了。怎麼樣找呢？在〈楞嚴咒〉有五種法。五種法裏有「息災法」，就是人有什麼災難，可以把它息了。有「吉祥法」，有不吉祥的事情，可以變成吉祥。有「勾召法」，就是妖魔鬼怪無論他離多遠，隨時可以把他捉來。又有「降伏法」，就是魔鬼他來了，你能降伏他。有這種的法，所以當時用那個〈楞嚴咒〉，把這個如意魔女，就給他叫來了，一叫來，一進門口的時候，她帶著一股臭氣，這股臭氣，腥臭得不得了。人一聞到那腥臭的氣就作嘔，就要嘔吐的那個樣子。

那她進來啦，就用她所煉的那個帽子，想用她這法寶，往我頭上來撇。一撇，這個帽子也撇不到我的頭上。那麼她這個帽子沒有用了，又拿出她這個圓圓的球想來打，也打不到我身上。

她兩種法寶都用了，都沒有功效，沒有用了。她在這個時候才知道是不行了，就要跑。要跑！東西南北，四維上下，什麼地方也跑不了。因為她一來的時候，我已經就結界，就好像擺上一個陣似的。那麼她沒有地方跑了；上邊也有人看著她，下邊也有人看著她，左右前後都有這護法天龍八部在這裏堵著她，跑不了。她跑不了，沒有法子，就跪下來。跪下，就哭起來了。

one can control her, but she has committed so many offenses there's bound to be someone who can subdue her. If she were to be destroyed, it would be a great pity, for she has cultivated diligently for many years. Even if she has enough power to kill me, I'll still save her. Finally, I must save all living beings in the world, and if I don't subdue her now, in the future many people will be harmed by her. For these three reasons, then, I'm going to work."

Just then the sheriff happened by and overheard us saying that the old woman was a demon. "No wonder!" he exclaimed. "That's why I was able to pick her up with one hand, just as if there were nothing there at all. It didn't occur to me at the time, but now I realize she's a demon."

We then had to find the demon. How did we do that? There are five kinds of dharmas in the Shurangama Mantra. One is the *dharma for extinguishing calamities*. If you are due to suffer a calamity, you can use this dharma to avert it. There is also the *dharma for creating auspiciousness*, which turns inauspicious events into auspicious ones. With the *dharma of summoning and hooking*, you can catch goblins, demons, and ghosts no matter how far away they are. There is also the *dharma of subduing and conquering*, which allows you to subdue any demon that comes. I employed these dharmas from the Shurangama Mantra to summon the As-You-Will demon woman.

When she entered the room, she had about her an intense and nauseating stench. She came in and tried to put her magic

137

當時，我就給她說法，說這個「四諦法」，說「十二因緣法」，又說這「六度法」，她即刻就明白了。明白了，她就要皈依三寶啦，發菩提心了。那麼這樣子呢，我就給她說了皈依，另給她起個名字，叫「金剛如意女」。皈依之後，她就常常跟著我到各處去度人。可是她的本性是一種魔性，無論到什麼地方，她都有著一股又臭又腥的味道；跟著我到什麼地方，都有這股的味道。以後我一看，她跟著我不行啦，我就把她派到吉林省蛟河縣磊法山「萬聖玲瓏洞」，到那地方去修行。

那個地方，怎麼叫「萬聖玲瓏洞」呢？我有很多奇奇怪怪的皈依弟子都派到那兒，都教他們在那地方修行。這個地方，我自己也到過這山上。那麼以後她修行很快就有了一點神通，常常到各處去救人去。不過她救人呢，也都不教人知道說是她怎麼樣救人。所謂：

> 善欲人見，不是真善；
> 惡恐人知，便是大惡。

你做的好事，願意教人知道，那不是真的好事。你做的壞事，怕人知道，那才是壞事。所以這個如意魔女，結果也變成一個佛的眷屬了。這個洞怎麼叫「萬聖玲瓏洞」？因為一個洞有三個洞門，在這邊可以看到

weapon—the black hat—on my head, but couldn't get it on me. Then she took out her round balls and tried to hit me, but they missed my body.

Both of her magic weapons had failed. Knowing she was finished, she turned to run, but when she first arrived, I had set up an invisible boundary that would trap her no matter where she tried to go. The gods, dragons, and others of the eightfold division of Dharma-protectors watched her from the left, right, front, rear, above, and below. Seeing that she couldn't get away, she knelt and wept.

I then spoke the Dharma for her. I explained the Four Noble Truths, the Twelve Causes and Conditions, and the Six Perfections. She immediately understood, resolved to realize Bodhi, and asked to take refuge with the Triple Jewel. I accepted her and gave her the name Vajra As-You-Will Maiden.

She followed me around to save people, but her basic make-up was that of a demon, and no matter where she went she carried her overwhelming stench. Seeing that it wouldn't do for her to follow me, I sent her to Leifa Mountain in Jiaohe County, Jilin Province, to cultivate in the Exquisite Cave of the Ten Thousand Saints. I have sent many of my strange and unusual disciples there to cultivate, and I have also been there myself. She cultivated vigorously and soon attained spiritual powers and could rescue people. When she rescued them, she didn't like it to be known,

139

那邊，那邊又可以看到這邊，玲瓏透體的那個樣子。好像這個玻璃杯裏面裝著什麼，一看就知道了，這叫玲瓏。不是一定說是glass（玻璃），就是裏邊可以看到外邊，外邊又可以看到裏邊。這一個洞有三個洞門，這三個洞門都互相通的，在那裏邊有一個廟。造這個廟的材料，都是用羊馱上去的。這一隻羊或者馱兩塊磚，或者一塊木頭，這麼用羊運上去的；因為那個山很高。

在那個洞裏邊，西邊這個洞門口，外邊又有一個「老君洞」——老子的洞。東邊這個洞門口，就有一個「滴水洞」。滴水洞那個洞裏，有這個水往下滴答滴答，這麼滴水。這個水啊，在那兒千人萬馬都夠吃的。後邊那個洞出去，就是「紀祖洞」。紀祖洞，就是紀曉堂。紀曉堂是我東北的人，他收過五個鬼，那麼他又在磊法山這兒，捉過這個黑魚精。這黑魚精是在明朝那時候，在北京作官的，叫黑大人。他姓黑，但是他不是個人，他是魚。那麼紀曉堂知道了，就要收拾他，知道他有一天就在這個山這兒過，那麼紀曉堂就在那兒等著他。等他從那兒過，紀曉堂會「掌手雷」，用掌手雷就把黑大人給打死在那個地方。

所以那山上的洞啊，誰也不知道有多少。你今天查有七十二個，明天就有七十三個，後天你再數，或者就

since good done hoping others will know is not true good, and evil done in secret for fear that others will know is truly great evil.

Thus, the former demon woman became one of the Buddha's followers.

Why is the cave called the "Exquisite Cave of the Ten Thousand Saints"? It's said to be exquisite because it has three entrances, which are mutually visible to each other. It's like a glass cup, in that one can see in from the outside and out from the inside. The three entrances to the cave are mutually connected. Inside the cave there is a temple made of bricks and lumber that were carried up the steep mountain crags on the backs of goats. One goat could carry two bricks or a piece of lumber at a time. Off the western entrance of the cave, there is another cave called the Cave of Lao Zi. Off the eastern entrance is the Dripping Water Cave, which drips enough water to satisfy a troop of ten thousand men and horses. The cave in the back is called the Cave of Patriarch Ji, named after Ji Xiaotang, a native of Manchuria who, in the Ming Dynasty, subdued five ghosts, one of whom was the Black Fish Spirit. The Black Fish Spirit was a Ming Dynasty official in Beijing called Blackie the Great. His last name was Black, but he wasn't a human; he was a fish. Ji Xiaotang knew this and was determined to capture him. He knew that "Blackie" would pass by the mountain one day, and so he waited for him. When he passed by, Ji Xiaotang released thunder from the palm of his hand and killed him.

No one actually knows how many caves there are in Leifa Mountain. Each time you count them, the number is

有七十個。總而言之，它沒有一定的數目。

有一個人到那個山上去，看見兩個老年人在那兒下棋。他在那兒看看，就咳嗽了一聲。咳嗽了一聲啊，這兩個有很長鬍子的老人一看，嘿！他怎麼來了？這個石頭自己有個門就關上了！他就在那跪著，一跪就跪死在那個地方。現在他的墳，還在那個石頭洞的門外邊。你看！人家求道、求法，跪死在那地方都不起來了。所以那個山有很多神仙。

我遇到一個李明福，他會武術，跑得才快呢！跑得像猴子那麼快。我到那個地方的時候，我也是一早起到山上去，一早大約四點多鐘到山上，就看到他在那兒拜佛，他後邊這個頭髮，束得有七、八斤重，頭上橛著一個簪，從來也不洗。他的面目很小的，小眼睛、小鼻子、小嘴巴、小臉，這麼很小的。但是他力量很大的，以前人家做鐵道，那個鐵道軌，八個人抬一條，他一個人可以拿兩條。一個人拿兩條，這麼一個胳臂夾一個，就這麼有力量。他叫李明福。究竟他多大年紀？什麼時候的人？沒有什麼人知道他。我到那兒遇到過這麼一個奇怪的人。

我對你們所講的，這不是講故事、不是自造的，這是實實在在，一個真實的事情！你們各位信呢，也可以；不信呢，也可以。信不信由你！

different—seventy-two today, seventy-three tomorrow, and m seventy the day after that.

A man once went there and saw two old men playing chess in a cave. When he coughed, the two long-bearded men said to themselves, "How did he get here?" and then the stone gate of the entrance closed by itself. The man knelt there seeking the truth from them until he finally died. His grave may still be seen outside the Stone Door Cave. How sincerely he sought for the truth!

There are many spirits and immortals up in the mountain. One was a man named Lee Mingfu, who had mastered kung fu and could run as fast as a monkey. Once I visited the cave at four in the morning and sawaybe him bowing to the Buddha. His hair, which he never washed, was held by a hairpin and matted in a lump that weighed five or six pounds. His facial features—eyes, nose, and mouth—and his body, were very small, but his body was strong. He alone could carry two railroad tracks so heavy that eight ordinary men would be needed to carry one; he would tuck one track under each arm. No one knew how old he was or where he was from. He was one of the strange men I met there.

These are not stories that I made up; they are true events. If you believe them, fine. If you don't believe, that's also fine. It's all up to you.

迴向偈

願以此功德　莊嚴佛淨土
上報四重恩　下濟三塗苦
若有見聞者　悉發菩提心
盡此一報身　同生極樂國

Verse of Transference

May the merit and virtue accrued from this work,
Adorn the Buddhas' Pure Lands,
Repaying four kinds of kindness above,
And aiding those suffering in the paths below.
May those who see and hear of this,
All bring forth the resolve for Bodhi,
And when this retribution body is over,
Be born together in the Land of Ultimate Bliss.

附錄

Appendix

辭彙解釋
Glossary

索引
Index

宣化上人簡傳
Biographical Sketch of the Venerable Master Hsuan Hua

宣化上人十八大願
The Eighteen Great Vows of the Venerable Master Hua

Glossary

Agama Sutras 阿含經 Agama is a Sanskrit word which means incomparable Dharma," for none of the heterodox teachings could compare to it. The Agama Sutras set forth the Small Vehicle teachings. The reference in the text to the *Avatamsaka* and the *Agama* is a general reference to the Five Periods of Shakyamuni Buddha's teachings:

1. The *Avatamaska Period*, likened to whole milk—raw and unprocessed, because it was so profound it was impossible for those of the Two Vehicles to assimilate;
2. The *Agama Period*, likened to skim milk—easy for youngsters to digest, representing that these teachings could be absorbed by those of the Two Vehicles;
3. The *Vaipulya Period*, Valipulya meaning "extensive," likened to curds, good for both youngsters and adults. The Vaipulya teachings contain a little of all the others periods, as they are aimed at expanding the minds of listeners;
4. The *Prajna Period*, likened to butter, suitable for adults.
5. The *Dharma Flower-Nirvana Period*, likened to clarified butter—the finest extract of milk.

Age Strong in Fighting and the Dharma-ending Age
鬥爭堅固時期 / 末法時期 There are Four Dharma Ages:

1. The *Age Strong in Liberation*. The first five hundred years during which a Buddha is in the world and many people certify to the Way and attain liberation. This is also known as the Proper Dharma Age.
2. The *Age Strong in Dhyana Samadhi*. The second five hundred years following a Buddha's passing into

148

Tranquillity. During this period many people gain certification through skill in meditation. This is also known as the Proper Dharma Age (a total of one thousand years).

3. The *Age Strong in Learning.* The third five hundred years (or a thousand years) during which many people investigate Sutras. This is also known as the Dharma-Image Age, because people are strong in building temples, monasteries, and images.

4. The *Age Strong in Fighting.* The fourth five hundred years (which continues on for tens of thousands of years) during which people fight. This is also known as theDharma-ending Age, and is the period we live in now.

Avatamsaka 華嚴 he title of the first Sutra all Buddhas speak upon enlightenment, the *Avatamsaka,* in Chinese, *Huayan,* is translated as "Flower Adornment."It is known as the "Sutraof the Dharma Realm." Also see *Agama* above.

blessings 福 The Sixth Patriarch describes blessings:

A confused person will foster blessings,
*   but not cultivate the Way*
And say, "To practice for the blessings
*   is practice of the Way."*
While giving and making offerings
*   brings blessings without limit,*
It is in the mind that the three evils
*   have their origin.*
By seeking blessings you may wish
*   to obliterate offenses*
But in the future, though you are blessed,
*   offenses still remain.*

Bodhisattva Way 菩薩道 A path of cultivation that involves benefiting, rescuing, and enlightening both oneself and all beings, the Bodhisattva Way is the foundation of the Great Vehicle (*Mahayana*) teaching and bases itself in Four Vast Vows:

1. Living beings are boundless, I vow to save them all.
2. Afflictions are endless, I vow to cut them all off.
3. Dharma-doors are infinite, I vow to study them all.
4. The Buddha Way is unsurpassed, I vow to realize it.

Brahma Heavens 梵天 These are the three heavens of the First Dhyana and are located in the Form Realm.

conditioned and unconditioned dharmas 有爲法 / 無爲法 In the *Hundred Dharmas Shastra,* conditioned dharmas include: (1) mind dharmas, (2) dharmas interactive with the mind, (3) form dharmas, and (4) dharmas not interactive with the mind. The last category of dharmas is (5) unconditioned harmas. Venerable Master Hua comments: "If one only knows about the first four kinds—conditioned dharmas, then one is an ordinary person or an externalist. If one knows the dharmas of the last category—unconditioned dharmas, then one resides in the one-sided emptiness of the Small Vehicle. The state of the Great Vehicle is that 'right in the midst of the conditioned is the unconditioned.'"

cultivation 修行 The practical application of the methods taught by the Buddha that lead to enlightenment.

Dharma 法 The teachings of the Buddha.

delusions of views and of thought 見惑 / 思惑 View delusions occur when one gives rise to greed and desire when confronted by states. There are eighty-eight categories of view delusions. Thought delusions occur when one is confused about principles and gives rise to discriminations. There are eight-one categories of thought delusions. The Venerable Master's commentary found on the *Flower Adornment Sutra Preface* says:

Arhats of the First Fruition have cut off eighty-eight grades of view delusions. Those of the Second Fruit have cut off the first six grades of thought delusion. When one testifies to the Third Fruit, one cuts off three more grades, and has severed nine grades of thought delusion in all. Fourth Fruit Arhats cut off all eighty-one grades of thought delusion in the Three Realms.

Dharma-body 法身 One of the three bodies of all Buddhas, which are:

1. the Dharma-body
2. the Reward-body
3. the Transformation-bodies

All living beings possess the potential to realize these three kinds of bodies.

Dharma Realm 法界 There are Four Kinds of Dharma Realms:

1. The Dharma Realm of Specifics
2. The Dharma Realm of Principle
3. The Dharma Realm of Non-Obstruction of Specifics and Principle
4. The Dharma Realm of Non-Obstruction of Specifics and Specifics

Further, there is division into Ten Dharma Realms, the topic of this text. The Ten Dharma Realms also are divided into Four Sagely

Dharma Realms and Six Common Dharma Realms (see index for listings).

dust 塵 Refers to the mundane world and to worldly passions. It is also sometimes used to refer to the six sense objects of forms, sounds, smells, tastes, objects of touch, and dharmas (mental objects).

emitting light and moving the earth 放光動地 These are two auspicious portents manifested by Buddhas.

Five Bhikshus 五比丘 The five people who accompanied the future Buddha when he went to the Himalayas to undertake ascetic practices in quest of enlightenment. The three who were relatives on Shakyamuni Buddha's father's side were: Asvajit ("Horse Victory"), Bhadrika ("Little Worthy"), and Mahanama Kulika. The two who were relatives on his mother's side were: Ajnatakaundinaya and Dashabala Kashyapa ("Drinker of Light").

five eyes and six spiritual penetrations 五眼六通 The five spiritual eyes are the flesh eye, the celestial eye, the Buddha eye, the wisdom eye, and the Dharma eye. The six spiritual penetrations are the penetration of the celestial eye, the penetration of the celestial ear, the penetration of others' thoughts, the penetration of past lives, the penetration of the complete spirit, and the penetration of the ending of outflows. Opening these five eyes and developing these six spiritual penetrations is a potential latent in all beings.

five precepts and ten good deeds 五戒十善 The five precepts are: no killing, no stealing, no sexual misconduct, no lying, and no taking of intoxicants (including drugs, cigarettes, etc.). The ten good deeds include three of the body: no killing, no stealing, and no sexual misconduct; four of the mouth: no harsh speech, no back-biting, no lying, and no frivolous speech; and three of the mind: no greed, no hatred, and no stupidity.

Ganges' sands 恆河沙數 The sands of the long and broad Ganges River in India were as fine as particles of wheat flour. Thus Shakyamuni Buddha often used them as an analogy for uncountable quantities.

good roots 善根 The roots of virtue that are planted during cultivation. Good roots grow out of faith. A quote from the *Avatamsaka Sutra* says, "Faith is the source of the Way and the mother of virtue, because it nourishes all good roots."

Great Vehicle 大乘 The *Mahayana* in Sanskrit, this is the vehicle of Bodhisattvas. The Great Vehicle teaching advocates bringing forth a resolve to save all living beings.

ignorance 無明 The fundamental affliction that plagues living beings. Buddhas are beings who have broken through ignorance.

karma 業 Deeds, activity; especially the deeds which we create ourselves and the retributions which those deeds bring upon us.

Kumarajiva, Dharma Master 鳩摩羅什法師 Of the Yao Qin dynasty in China, this Indian Dharma Master was a prolific translator of Buddhist Sutras from Sanskrit to Chinese. His mother's decision to become a Buddhist nun influenced her son to also leave the home-life. Dharma Master Kumarajiva established a translation center in Chang An, the capital city at that time, and translated over three hundred volumes of Sutra texts.

Mahaprajnaparamita 摩訶般若波羅密 A Sanskrit term that translates as "great wisdom that has arrived at the other shore"—the perfection of wisdom.

merit and virtue 功德 The Sixth Patriarch defines this as: "Merit and virtue are in the Dharma-body, not in the cultivation of blessings. Seeing your own nature is merit, and equanimity is virtue. To be unobstructed in every thought, constantly seeing the true, wonderful function of your original nature is called merit and virtue. Inner humility is merit, and the reverence is virtue. Your self-nature establishing the outer practice of reverence is virtue. Your self-nature establishing the myriad dharmas is merit, and the mind apart from thought is virtue. Not being separated from the self-nature is merit, and the correct use of the undefiled self-nature is virtue."

outflows 漏 All bad habits and faults are outflows. Outflows are the root of birth and death; they let our vital energy leak away.

Sangha 僧伽 The community of Buddhist monks and nuns.

Sutra 經 Discourses by the Buddha or by various members of the assembly with the authority of the Buddha.

Shurangama Mantra 楞嚴咒 The longest and most powerful mantra in Buddhism. Shurangama means "ultimately firm and solid."

six periods of the day and night 晝夜六時 This simply means all the time.

Small Vehicle 小乘 Also referred to as the Two Vehicles, this includes the vehicle of Those Enlightened to Conditions and the Hearers.

Tathagata 如來 One of the Ten Titles assigned to all Buddhas, this Sanskrit word is interpreted in English as "Thus Come One." The word actually can be construed to mean "not come" and "not gone," describing the state of Buddhas, who, as fully enlightened beings, are beyond birth and death.

three periods of time 三世 The past, the present, and the future.

yin and yang 陰陽 Yang is the male principle and is represented by light, heaven. Yin in the female principle and is represented by darkness, the earth. They are the fundamental duality from which all other dualities arise.

The Way 道 The spiritual path of cultivation; the ultimate truth, which is realized through following that path.

Way-place 道場 A monastery; a place where enlightenment is sought and attained.

Index

A

Agama Sutras, 45

Age Strong in Fighting, 77

Ajnatakaundinya, Venerable

    as King Kali, 51
    name defined, 53
    one of five Bhikshus, 43

animals

    Dharma Realm of, 89

Arhat sandals with no socks, 117

Arhats

    see Hearers, 43

arrogance

    lack of, 13

As-You-Wish Woman, 113

Ashvajit

    one of five Bhikshus, 43

asuras

    Dharma Realm of, 71

authority, 75

B

Black Fish Spirit, 141

blessings, 23, 65, 75

Bodhisattvas

    Dharma Realm of, 19
    of the provisional teaching, 55
    two meanings of, 19

bowing to the Buddhas, 143

    merit and virtue from, 21

Buddhas, 5

    Dharma Realm of, 9
    emit light, 15
    people becoming, 21

C

cause and effect, 101

caves

    of Leifa Mountain, 141

conditioned dharmas, 33

Confucius

    quote about ghosts and spirits, 99

consequences of own actions,
85

contention, 15

cultivation, 25, 139

D

delusions

of views, thought, and dust
and sand, 43

demons, 65

depression, 105

Dharma

merit from listening to, 21
spoken for a demon, 139

Dharma Realm, 7

of animals, 89
of asuras, 71
of Bodhisattvas, 19
of Buddhas, 9
of gods, 59
of Hearers, 41
of hell-beings, 105
of hungry ghosts, 97
of people, 81
of Those Enlightened to
Conditions, 31

Dharma-body, 13, 111

Dharma-ending Age, 77

Dharma-protecting spirits, 51

disciples

strange and unusual, 139

Du Shun, Patriarch

feet not touch the ground, 41

E

ego, 13

Enlightened to Conditions,
Those

Dharma Realm of, 31

enlightenment, 111

expedience, 55

Exquisite Cave of the Ten
Thousand Saints, 139

F

feet not touch the ground

sign of sagehood, 41

fighting, 77

five Bhikshus, 43

five eyes, 119

宣化上人簡傳

宣公上人，東北吉林省雙城縣人，民初戊午年農曆三月十六日生。俗姓白，名玉書，又名玉禧。父富海公，一生勤儉治家，以務農為業。母胡太夫人，生前茹素念佛，數十年如一日，懷上人時曾向佛菩薩祈願，生上人前夕，夢見阿彌陀佛大放光明，遂生上人。

上人生性沉默寡言，天賦俠義心腸，幼年即隨母親茹素念佛。年十一，見鄰居一死嬰，感生死事大，無常迅速，毅然有出家之志。十二歲，聞雙城王孝子——常仁大師，盡孝得道，發願效法。懺悔過去不孝父母，決定每日早晚向父母叩頭認錯，以報親恩，自此漸以孝行見稱，人稱「白孝子」。

十五歲皈依^上常^下智老和尚為師。同年入學，於四書五經、諸子百家、醫卜星相等，無不貫通。求學期間，參加道德會等慈善團體；又為不識字者，講《六祖壇經》、《金剛經》等；為貧寒者，創辦義務學校。

十九歲母親逝世，遂禮請三緣寺^上常^下智老和尚為剃度，法名安慈，字度輪。並披緇結廬於母親墓旁，守孝

Biographical Sketch of the Venerable Master Hsuan Hua

The Venerable Master, a native of Shuangcheng County in Jilin Province of China, was born on the sixteenth day of the third lunar month in the year of *wuwu* at the beginning of the century. He was named Yushu (or Yuxi) Bai. His father, Fuhai Bai, was hardworking and thrifty. His mother, maiden name Hu, ate only vegetarian food and recited the Buddha's name every day. When she was pregnant with the Master, she prayed to the Buddhas and Bodhisattvas. The night before his birth, in a dream she saw Amitabha Buddha emitting brilliant light. Following that the Master was born.

The Master was quiet and untalkative by nature, but he had a righteous and heroic spirit. As a child, he followed his mother's example and ate only vegetarian food and recited the Buddha's name. At the age of eleven, the sight of a dead infant made him aware of the great matter of birth and death, and he resolved to leave the home-life. At twelve, he heard of how Filial Son Wong (Great Master Chang Ren) of Shuangcheng County had practiced filial piety and attained the Way, and he vowed to follow the Filial Son's example. The Master decided to bow to his parents every morning and evening as a way of acknowledging his faults and repaying his parents' kindness. Because of his filial piety, he became known as Filial Son Bai.

At fifteen, he took refuge under the Venerable Master Chang Zhi. That year he began to attend school and mastered the Four Books, the Five Classics, the texts of various Chinese schools of thought, and the fields of medicine, divination, astrology, and physiognomy. He participated in the Virtue Society and other charitable societies. He explained the *Sixth Patriarch's Sutra*, the *Vajra Sutra*, and other Sutras to those who were illiterate, and he started a free school for the poor.

When he was nineteen, his mother passed away, and he requested Venerable Master Chang Zhi of Sanyuan (Three Conditions) Monastery to shave his head. He was given the Dharma name An Tse and style name To Lun. Dressed in the left-home robes, he built a simple hut by his mother's grave and lived there for three years in observance of filial piety. During that period,

163

期間，發十八大願，拜華嚴、禮淨懺、修禪定、習教
觀、日一食、夜不臥，功夫日純，得鄉里人民之愛戴
禮敬，其洗鍊精虔，感動諸佛菩薩、護法龍天，故靈
異之事多不勝數，人稱奇僧。

一日打坐，見六祖大師至茅棚，告曰：「將來你會到
西方，所遇之人無量無邊，教化眾生，如恆河沙，不
可悉數，此是西方佛法崛起之徵象。」言畢，忽而不
見。守孝期滿，隱居於長白山支脈彌陀洞內修苦行。
後回三緣寺，爲首座。居東北期間，觀機逗教，點化
迷萌，濟世活人，感化無量龍蛇、狐狸、鬼神，求皈
受戒，改惡修善。

一九四六年，慕虛雲老和尚爲宗門泰斗，遂束裝就道
，前往參禮。途中備經艱苦，蹤跡遍及內陸各大梵剎
，一九四七年赴普陀山受具足戒，一九四八年抵廣州
曹溪南華寺，禮虛雲老和尚，受命任南華寺戒律學院
監學，後轉任教務主任。雲公觀其爲法門龍象，乃傳
授法脈，賜法號宣化，遂爲溈仰宗第九代接法人，摩
訶迦葉初祖傳承之第四十五代。

一九四九年，叩別虛雲老和尚，赴香港弘法，闡揚禪
、教、律、密、淨五宗並重，打破門戶之見。並重建
古剎、印經造像，成立西樂園寺、慈興禪寺、佛教講

he made eighteen great vows. He bowed to the *Flower Adornment Sutra*, engaged in worship and repentance, practiced meditation, studied the scriptures, ate only one meal a day, and did not lie down to sleep at night. His sincere efforts to purify and cultivate himself won the admiration of the villagers and evoked numerous miracles and responses from the Buddhas, Bodhisattvas, and Dharma-protecting gods and dragons. He came to be known as an extraordinary monk.

One day as he was sitting in meditation, he saw the Great Master, the Sixth Patriarch, come to his hut and tell him, "In the future you will go to the West and meet countless people. The living beings you teach and transform will be as countless as the sands of the Ganges River. That will mark the beginning of the Buddhadharma in the West." After saying that, the Sixth Patriarch vanished. The Master completed his observance of filial piety and went to Changbai Mountain, where he dwelled in seclusion and practiced austerities at the Amitabha Cave. Later he returned to Sanyuan Monastery and became the leader of the assembly. During his years in Manchuria, the Master taught people according to their potentials. He awakened those who were confused and saved many lives. Countless dragons, snakes, foxes, ghosts, and spirits took refuge and received the precepts from him, changing their evil and cultivating goodness.

In 1946, the Master embarked on an arduous journey to Caoxi, Guangzhou, to pay homage to the Elder Master Hsu Yun, whom he esteemed as a great hero of Buddhism. Along the way he stayed at many renowned monasteries in China and received complete ordination at Mount Putuo in 1947. He reached Nanhua Monastery in 1948 and paid homage to Elder Master Hsu Yun. The Elder Master appointed him as an instructor and later as the Dean of Academic Affairs in the Nanhua Vinaya Academy. He saw that the Master was an outstanding individual and transmitted the Dharma to him, giving him the Dharma name Hsuan Hua and making him the Ninth Patriarch of the Wei Yang Sect, the forty-fifth generation since the First Patriarch Mahakashyapa.

In 1949, the Master bid farewell to the Elder Master Yun and went to Hong Kong. In propagating the Dharma there, he emphasized all five schools of Buddhism—Chan, Doctrine, Vinaya, Esoteric, and Pure Land. He renovated old temples, printed Sutras, and constructed images. Among the temples he established were Western Bliss Gardens Monastery, Cixing Chan Monastery,

165

堂。居港十餘年間，應眾生懇請，普結法緣，相繼開講《地藏經》、《金剛經》、《彌陀經》、《楞嚴經》、《普門品》等經典多部，舉辦《大悲懺》、《藥師懺》、佛七、禪七等法會，又創辦《心法》雜誌等，終日爲弘揚大法而奔忙，使佛法大興於香江。其間亦曾數度赴泰國、緬甸等地，考察南傳佛教，志欲溝通大小乘，以團結佛教力量。

一九五九年，師觀察西方機緣成熟，爲將佛教之眞實義理傳播至世界各地，遂令弟子在美成立中美佛教總會（法界佛教總會前身）。一九六一年，赴澳洲弘法一年，以機緣未熟，一九六二年返港。同年應美國佛教人士邀請，隻身赴美，樹正法幢於三藩市佛教講堂。初住無窗潮濕之地窖，猶如墳墓，故自號「墓中僧」。時值美蘇兩國有古巴飛彈危機之事，爲求戰爭不起，世界和平，故絕食五星期。絕食畢，危機遂解。

一九六八年，成立暑假楞嚴講修班，有華盛頓州州立大學學生三十餘人，遠來學習佛法。結業後，美籍青年五人，懇求剃度出家，創美國佛教史始有僧相之記錄。此後，上人致力於弘法、譯經、教育等事業，又廣收徒眾、建道場、立宗旨。集四眾之眞誠，盡未來際劫，遍虛空法界，光大如來正法家業。

and the Buddhist Lecture Hall. During a period of over ten years, he created extensive Dharma-affinities with the people of Hong Kong. The Sutras he lectured on included the *Earth Store Sutra*, the *Vajra Sutra*, the *Amitabha Sutra*, the *Shurangama Sutra*, and the "Universal Door Chapter" of the *Dharma Flower Sutra*. He held such Dharma assemblies as the Great Compassion Repentance, the Medicine Master Repentance, and recitation and meditation sessions. He published the magazine *Hsin Fa (Mind Dharma)*. As a result of his zealous efforts to propagate the Dharma, Buddhism flourished in Hong Kong. During that time he also visited such countries as Thailand and Burma to study Theravada Buddhism. He hoped to establish communication between the Mahayana and the Theravada traditions and to unite the different sects of Buddhism.

In 1959, the Master saw that conditions were ripe in the West, and he instructed his disciples to establish the Sino-American Buddhist Association (later renamed the Dharma Realm Buddhist Association) in the United States. In 1961 he traveled to Australia and preached the Dharma for one year. Since the conditions were not yet ripe there, he returned to Hong Kong in 1962. Later that year, at the invitation of Buddhists in America, the Master traveled alone to the United States and raised the banner of the Proper Dharma at the Buddhist Lecture Hall in San Francisco. Living in a damp, windowless basement that resembled a grave, he called himself "The Monk in the Grave." When the Cuban Missile Crisis broke out, the Master embarked on a thirty-five-day fast to pray for an end to hostilities and for world peace. By the end of his fast, the crisis had been resolved.

During the Shurangama Study and Practice Summer Session in 1968, over thirty students from the University of Washington in Seattle went to San Francisco to study with the Master. At the end of the session, five of them requested permission to shave their heads and leave the home-life. That was the beginning of the Sangha in the history of American Buddhism. The Master devoted himself to propagating the Dharma, directing the translation of the Buddhist Canon, and developing education. He accepted many disciples, established monasteries, and set forth principles. He exhorted his disciples to work hard in order to cause the Proper Dharma to flourish eternally throughout the Dharma Realm.

在弘法方面，上人講經說法，深入淺出，數十年如一日，並極力栽培四眾弘法人才，多次率團至各大學及世界各國弘法訪問，以期引導眾生改惡向善，開啓本有的智慧。

在譯經方面，現已有百餘本譯爲英文。另有西班牙文、越南文、日文等譯本，預計將《大藏經》譯成各國文字，使佛法傳遍寰宇。

在教育方面，萬佛聖城設有育良小學、培德中學、法界佛教大學、僧伽居士訓練班等教育機構，分支道場亦附設周末、周日班學校。以孝、悌、忠、信、禮、義、廉恥八德爲做人基礎，以大公無私、慈悲喜捨爲究竟目標。男女分校，義務教學，培養品格高尚之人才，以期利益世界人類。

上人教導弟子天天參禪打坐、念佛、拜懺、研究經典、嚴持戒律、日中一食、衣不離體，和合共住，互相砥礪，在西方建立行持正法之僧團，以圖匡扶正教，令正法久住。又開放萬佛聖城爲國際性宗教中心，提倡團結世界宗教，大家互相學習，溝通合作，共同追求眞理，爲世界和平而努力。

上人一生大公無私，發願代眾生受一切苦難，將己身一切福樂迴向法界眾生，難行能行，難忍能忍，其堅貞之志節

The Master lectured on the Sutras and spoke the Dharma every day for several decades, explaining profound principles in a way that made them easy to understand. He also trained his left-home and lay disciples to explain the teachings. He led various delegations to disseminate the Dharma at various universities and in various countries around the world, with the aim of leading beings to turn toward goodness and to discover their innate wisdom.

To date over a hundred volumes of the Master's explanations of the scriptures have been translated into English, and some have also been translated into Spanish, Vietnamese, and other languages. The Master's aim is to translate the Buddhist Canon into all the world's languages so that the Dharma will become popular worldwide.

The Master established Instilling Goodness Elementary School, Developing Virtue Secondary School, Dharma Realm Buddhist University, and the Sangha and Laity Training Programs at the City of Ten Thousand Buddhas. Many of the branch monasteries of Dharma Realm Buddhist Association have classes for children as well. These educational programs are based on the eight virtues of filiality, fraternal respect, loyalty, trustworthiness, propriety, righteousness, incorruptibility, and a sense of shame. In order to encourage students to develop the virtues of kindness, compassion, joy, and charity and to educate them to become men and women of integrity who will be able to contribute to society, the boys and girls study separately and the volunteer teachers regard education as their personal responsibility.

The Master taught his disciples to meditate, recite the Buddha's name, practice repentance, study the Sutras, and observe the precepts strictly. He taught them to eat only one meal a day (at midday) and to always wear the precept sash. He taught them to dwell in harmony and to encourage each other. Under his guidance, a Sangha that practices and maintains the Proper Dharma has grown up in the West. The Master established the City of Ten Thousand Buddhas as an international spiritual community where students and truth-seekers can study and work together for the cause of world peace and harmony among religions.

The Master's life was one of total selflessness. He vowed to take the suffering and hardships of all living beings upon himself, and to dedicate to them

169

，堪爲疾風中之勁燭，烈火內之精金。上人曾撰一聯以明
其志：

> 凍死不攀緣，
> 餓死不化緣，
> 窮死不求緣。
> 隨緣不變，不變隨緣，
> 抱定我們三大宗旨。
>
> 捨命爲佛事，
> 造命爲本事，
> 正命爲僧事。
> 即事明理，明理即事，
> 推行祖師一脈心傳。

又堅守一生奉行之六大宗旨：不爭、不貪、不求、不
自私、不自利、不打妄語，利益群生；以慈悲智慧之
敎化，捨己爲人。其以身作則之精神，令無數人眞誠
改過，走向清淨光明之菩提大道。

今以眾生障深福薄，一代聖人遽爾示寂，娑婆眾生頓
失依怙；然上人之一生即是一部法界的華嚴大經，雖
示現涅槃，而恆轉無盡法輪——不留痕跡，從虛空來
，回到虛空去。弟子眾等唯有謹遵師敎，抱定宗旨，在
菩薩道上精進不懈，以期報上人浩瀚之深恩於萬一。

all the blessings and happiness that he himself ought to enjoy. He practiced what was difficult to practice and endured what was difficult to endure. No amount of hardship could deter him from fulfilling his lofty resolves. He composed a verse expressing his principles:

Freezing, we do not scheme.
Starving, we do not beg.
Dying of poverty, we ask for nothing.
According with conditions, we do not change.
Not changing, we accord with conditions.
We adhere firmly to our three great principles.

We renounce our lives to do the Buddha's work.
We take the responsibility to mold our own destinies.
We rectify our lives as the Sangha's work.
Encountering specific matters,
* we understand the principles.*
Understanding the principles, we apply
* them in specific matters.*
We carry on the single pulse of the patriarchs'
* mind-transmission.*

Through his unwavering maintenance of the six guiding principles of not fighting, not being greedy, not seeking, not being selfish, not pursuing personal advantage, and not lying, he brought benefit to many. He dedicated himself to serving others and taught them with wisdom and compassion. His personal example influenced countless people to change their faults and to walk upon the pure, bright path to enlightenment.

Although the Master manifested entry into Nirvana on June 7, 1995 (the tenth day of the fifth lunar month), he constantly turns the infinite Dharma wheel. He came from empty space and returned to empty space without leaving a trace. The least we can do in return for the Master's deep and profound kindness is to carefully follow his teachings, hold to our principles, and advance vigorously toward Bodhi.

宣化上人十八大願

一、願盡虛空、遍法界、十方三世一切菩薩等，若有一未成佛時，我誓不取正覺。

二、願盡虛空、遍法界、十方三世一切緣覺等，若有一未成佛時，我誓不取正覺。

三、願盡虛空、遍法界、十方三世一切聲聞等，若有一未成佛時，我誓不取正覺。

四、願三界諸天人等，若有一未成佛時，我誓不取正覺。

五、願十方世界一切人等，若有一未成佛時，我誓不取正覺。

六、願天、人、一切阿修羅等，若有一未成佛時，我誓不取正覺。

七、願一切畜生界等，若有一未成佛時，我誓不取正覺。

The Eighteen Great Vows of the Venerable Master Hua

1. I vow that as long as there is a single Bodhisattva in the three periods of time throughout the ten directions of the Dharma Realm, to the very end of empty space, who has not accomplished Buddhahood, I too will not attain the right enlightenment.

2. I vow that as long as there is a single Pratyekabuddha in the three periods of time throughout the ten directions of the Dharma Realm, to the very end of empty space, who has not accomplished Buddhahood, I too will not attain the right enlightenment.

3. I vow that as long as there is a single Shravaka in the three periods of time throughout the ten directions of the Dharma Realm, to the very end of empty space, who has not accomplished Buddhahood, I too will not attain the right enlightenment.

4. I vow that as long as there is a single god in the Triple Realm who has not accomplished Buddhahood, I too will not attain the right enlightenment.

5. I vow that as long as there is a single human being in the worlds of the ten directions who has not accomplished Buddhahood, I too will not attain the right enlightenment.

6. I vow that as long as there is a single asura who has not accomplished Buddhahood, I too will not attain the right enlightenment.

7. I vow that as long as there is a single animal who has not accomplished Buddhahood, I too will not attain the right enlightenment.

八、願一切餓鬼界等，若有一未成佛時，我誓不取正
　　覺。

九、願一切地獄界等，若有一未成佛，或地獄不空時
　　，我誓不取正覺。

一十、願凡是三界諸天、仙、人、阿修羅，飛潛動植
　　　、靈界龍畜、鬼神等眾，曾經皈依
　　　我者，若有一未成佛時，我誓不取正覺。

十一、願將我所應享受一切福樂，悉皆迴向，普施法
　　　界眾生。

十二、願將法界眾生所有一切苦難，悉皆與我一人代
　　　受。

十三、願分靈無數，普入一切不信佛法眾生心，令其
　　　改惡向善，悔過自新，皈依三寶，究竟作佛。

十四、願一切眾生，見我面，乃至聞我名，悉發菩提
　　　心，速得成佛道。

十五、願恪遵佛制，實行日中一食。

8. I vow that as long as there is a single hungry ghost who has not accomplished Buddhahood, I too will not attain the right enlightenment.

9. I vow that as long as there is a single hell-dweller who has not accomplished Buddhahood, I too will not attain the right enlightenment.

10. I vow that as long as there is a single god, immortal, human, asura, air-bound or water-bound creature, animate or inanimate object, or a single dragon, beast, ghost, or spirit, and so forth, of the spiritual realm that has taken refuge with me and has not accomplished Buddhahood, I too will not attain the right enlightenment.

11. I vow to fully dedicate all blessings and bliss which I ought myself receive and enjoy to all living beings of the Dharma Realm.

12. I vow to fully take upon myself all sufferings and hardships of all the living beings in the Dharma Realm.

13. I vow to manifest innumerable bodies as a means to gain access into the minds of living beings throughout the universe who do not believe in the Buddhadharma, causing them to correct their faults and tend toward wholesomeness, repent of their errors and start anew, take refuge in the Triple Jewel, and ultimately accomplish Buddhahood.

14. I vow that all living beings who see my face or even hear my name will bring forth the Bodhi resolve and quickly accomplish Buddhahood.

15. I vow to respectfully observe the Buddha's instructions and cultivate the practice of eating only one meal per day.

十六、願覺諸有情，普攝群機。

十七、願此生即得五眼六通，飛行自在。

十八、願一切求願，必獲滿足。

結云：

　　　眾生無邊誓願度，
　　　煩惱無盡誓願斷，
　　　法門無量誓願學，
　　　佛道無上誓願成。

16. I vow to enlighten all sentient beings, universally responding to the multitude of differing potentials.

17. I vow to obtain the five eyes, six spiritual powers, and the freedom of being able to fly in this very life.

18. I vow that all of my vows will certainly be fulfilled.

Conclusion:

I vow to save the innumerable living beings.
I vow to eradicate the inexhaustible afflictions.
I vow to study the illimitable Dharma-doors.
I vow to accomplish the unsurpassed Buddha Way.

南無護法韋馱菩薩

Namo Dharma Protector Wei Tuo Bodhisattva

DHARMA REALM BUDDHIST ASSOCIATION
BUDDHIST TEXT TRANSLATION SOCIETY
PUBLICATIONS

法界佛教總會
佛經翻譯委員會

Chinese/English Buddhist Books & Tapes
中／英文佛經叢書、錄音帶目錄

Buddhist Text Translation Society Publications

Buddhist Text Translation Society
International Translation Institute
1777 Murchison Drive
Burlingame, California 94010-4504
Phone: 415-692-5912; Fax: 415-692-5056

When Buddhism first came to China from India, one of the most important tasks required for its establishment was the translation of the Buddhist scriptures from Sanskrit into Chinese. This work involved a great many people, such as the renowned monk National Master Kumarajiva (fifth century), who led an assembly of over 800 people to work on the translation of the Tripitaka (Buddhist canon) for over a decade. Because of the work of individuals such as these, nearly the entire Buddhist Tripitaka of over a thousand texts exists to the present day in Chinese.

Now the banner of the Buddha's Teachings is being firmly planted in Western soil, and the same translation work is being done from Chinese into English. Since 1970, the Buddhist Text Translation Society (BTTS) has been making a paramount contribution toward this goal. Aware that the Buddhist Tripitaka is a work of such magnitude that its translation could never be entrusted to a single person, the BTTS, emulating the translation assemblies of ancient times, does not publish a work until it has passed through four committees for primary translation, revision, editing, and certification. The leaders of these committees are Bhikshus (monks) and Bhikshunis (nuns) who have devoted their lives to the study and practice of the Buddha's teachings. For this reason, all of the works of the BTTS put an emphasis on what the principles of the Buddha's teachings mean in terms of actual practice and not simply hypothetical conjecture.

The translations of canonical works by the Buddhist Text Translation Society are accompanied by extensive commentaries by the Venerable Tripitaka Master Hsuan Hua and are available in softcover only unless otherwise noted.

Buddhist Sutras

Amitabha Sutra. This Sutra, which was spoken by the Buddha without having been formally requested as other Sutras were, explains the causes and circumstances for rebirth in the Land of Ultimate Bliss of Amitabha (Limitless Light) Buddha. The commentary includes extensive information on common Buddhist terminology and stories about many of the Buddha's foremost disciples. ISBN 0-917512-01-4. 204 pgs. $8.00.

(Explicación General del Sutra en que El Buda Habla de Amitabha. Spanish edition. ISBN 0-917512-30-6. $8.00.)

Dharma Flower (Lotus) Sutra. In this Sutra, which was spoken in the last period of the Buddha's teaching, the Buddha proclaims the ultimate principles of the Dharma, which unite all previous teachings into one. When completed, the translation of the entire Sutra and commentary will comprise an estimated fifteen to twenty volumes. The following are those volumes that have been published to date. Set of ten volumes, $79.50.

Volume I. Foreword by Venerable Master Hua. Discusses the five periods and the eight teachings of the T'ien T'ai School and then analyzes the School's Five Profound Meanings as they relate to the Sutra. The last portion tells of the life of Tripitaka Master Kumarajiva, who translated the Sutra from Sanskrit into Chinese. ISBN 0-917512-16-2. 85 pgs.

Volume II. Chapter One, Introduction. Describes the setting for the speaking of the Sutra, the assembly that gathered to hear it, the Buddha's emission of light, the questions asked by Maitreya Bodhisattva, and the response given by Manjushri Bodhisattva. ISBN 0-917512-22-7. 324 pgs.

Volume III. Chapter Two, Expedient Methods. After the Buddha emerges from samadhi, he speaks of the vast merit and virtue of the Buddhas. Shariputra beseeches him to expound further on this. After his third request, the Buddha consents and for the first time proclaims that

all beings without exception can become Buddhas.
ISBN 0-917512-26-X. 183 pgs.

Volume IV. Chapter Three, A Parable. The Buddha explains the purpose of his teachings by means of an analogy of an elder who tries to rescue five hundred children who are absorbed in play in a burning house. ISBN 0-917512-62-6. 371 pgs.

Volume V. Chapter Four, Belief and Understanding. Four of the Buddha's foremost Arhat disciples relate a parable about a prodigal son to express their joy upon hearing that they, too, can become Buddhas in the future. ISBN 0-917512-64-2. 200 pgs.

Volume VI. Chapter Five, Medicinal Herbs and **Chapter Six, Conferring Predictions.** The Buddha uses the analogy of a rain cloud to illustrate how his teaching benefits all beings with total impartiality. He also predicts that the previously mentioned Arhat disciples will become Buddhas in the future. In bestowing his prediction, he tells what their future Buddha names will be and what the names of their world systems and *kalpas* will be, as well as the scope of their Dharma. ISBN 0-917512-65-0. 161 pgs.

Volume VII. Chapter Seven, Parable of the Transformation City. The Buddha teaches that the attainment of his Arhat disciples is like a city that he conjured up as an expedient when they became weary of the journey to Buddhahood. ISBN 0-917512-67-7. 250 pgs.

Volume VIII. Chapter Eight, Five Hundred Disciples Receive Predictions and **Chapter Nine, Bestowing Predictions upon Those Studying and Beyond Study.** More than a thousand disciples receive predictions that they will become Buddhas in the future. ISBN 0-917512-71-5. 160 pgs.

Volume IX. Chapter Ten, Masters of the Dharma and **Chapter Eleven, Vision of the Jewelled Stupa.** Chapter Ten explains the vast merit from upholding and propagating the *Wonderful Dharma Lotus Flower Sutra.* In Chapter Eleven, all of the many millions of transformation bodies of Shakyamuni Buddha gather in one place so that those in the assembly can see Many Jewels Buddha, who in the distant past made a vow to appear wherever this Sutra is spoken. ISBN 0-917512-85-5. 270 pgs.

Volume X. Chapter Twelve, Devadatta and **Chapter Thirteen, Exhortation to Maintain.** In Chapter Twelve, the Buddha reveals that Devadatta was once his teacher in a former life, and then bestows a prediction of Buddhahood on him. The eight-year-old dragon girl becomes a Buddha. In Chapter Thirteen, the Buddha bestows predictions of Buddhahood on Bhikshunis. ISBN 0-917512-52-9. 150 pgs.

Flower Adornment (Avatamsaka) Sutra. Known as the "King of Kings" of all Buddhist scriptures because of its profundity and great length (81 rolls containing more than 700,000 Chinese characters), this Sutra contains the most complete explanation of the Buddha's state and the Bodhisattva's quest for Awakening. When completed, the entire Sutra text with commentary will comprise from 75 to 100 volumes. The following are those volumes that have been published to date:

Verse Preface. A succinct and eloquent verse commentary by T'ang Dynasty National Master Ch'ing Liang, the Master of seven emperors. The Preface gives a complete explanation of all the fundamental principles contained in the Sutra. This is the first English translation of this text. Bilingual edition, English/Chinese. ISBN 0-917512-28-6. 244 pgs. $7.00.

Prologue. A detailed explanation of the principles of the Sutra, by National Master Ch'ing Liang, utilizing the Hsien Shou method of analyzing scriptures known as the Ten Doors. The *Prologue* contains the first Nine Doors. Will be approximately seven to ten volumes upon completion. Set of four books, $38.00. The following volumes have been published to date:

> **First Door. The Causes and Conditions for the Arising of the Teaching** of the *Flower Adornment Sutra*. Complete in one volume. ISBN 0-917512-66-9. 252 pgs.
>
> **Second Door. The Stores and Teachings in Which It Is Contained.** Three volumes as follows:
>
> > **Part One.** Complete discussion of the Three Stores. Beginning of discussion of the Schools in China.
> > ISBN 0-917512-73-1. 280 pgs.
> >
> > **Part Two.** More on Chinese schools. The Indian schools and comparisons between them.
> > ISBN 0-917512-98-7. 220 pgs.
> >
> > **Part Three.** Detailed discussion of the Five Hsien Shou Teachings, the sequence of the Teaching Methods, and the inconceivable state of the Flower Adornment. Completes the explanation of the Second Door.
> > ISBN 0-88139-009-7. 160 pgs.

The following twenty-two volumes are available as a set only. $174.50.

Flower Store Adorned Sea of Worlds, Chapter Five, Parts One & Two. Describes the universe we live in, including an explanation of principles pertaining to the coming into being of worlds, the wind wheels that uphold them, their orbits, and their mutual attraction. Also, detailed descriptions of the worlds located on the twenty tiers of the lotus that forms the basis of our cosmic structure.
ISBN 0-917512-54-5. 250 pgs.

Flower Store Adorned Sea of Worlds, Chapter Five, Part Three, and Vairochana, Chapter Six. Conclusion of Chapter Five, "Flower Store Adorned Sea of Worlds," and Chapter Six, "Vairochana," which discusses the causes and conditions of the clear, pure Dharma-body Buddha, Vairochana Buddha. ISBN 0-88139-114-X. 191 pgs.

The Names of the Thus Come Ones, Chapter Seven, and **The Four Holy Truths,Chapter Eight.** In Chapter Seven, the Bodhisattvas gather from the worlds of the ten directions to request that the Buddha speak about the Great Bodhisattva practices, which are explained at great length in later chapters of the *Flower Adornment Sutra.* In Chapter Eight, each of the Four Holy Truths—suffering, accumulation, extinction, and the Way—are explained according to the conditions of ten different worlds plus the Saha World, the world that we inhabit. ISBN 0-88139-014-3. 77 pgs.

Bright Enlightenment, Chapter Nine. From the soles of his feet, Shakyamuni Buddha emits light, which continually gets brighter and shines upon more and more different countries in the ten directions. After each time that he emits light, Manjushri Bodhisattva speaks verses praising the virtues of the Buddha. ISBN 0-88139-005-4. 225 pgs.

Pure Conduct, Chapter Eleven. This chapter of the Sutra gives a detailed explanation of the pure practices of the Bodhisattva. It is one of the most renowned guides to the Vinaya in the Buddhist canon. ISBN 0-917512-37-5. 255 pgs.

Ten Dwellings, Chapter Fifteen. Explains the state of the Ten Dwellings attained by the Bodhisattva. ISBN 0-917512-77-4. 185 pgs.

Brahma Conduct, Chapter Sixteen. Explains the meanings of the pure Brahma conduct cultivated by the Bodhisattva.
ISBN 0-917512-80-4. 65 pgs.

The Merit and Virtue from First Bringing forth the Mind, Chapter Seventeen. Uses various analogies to describe the merit obtained by the Bodhisattva when he first resolves his mind on becoming enlightened.
ISBN 0-917512-83-9. 200 pgs.

The Ten Inexhaustible Treasuries, Chapter Twenty-two. Explains the Ten Inexhaustible Treasuries attained by the Bodhisattva immediately following the Ten Conducts.
ISBN 0-917512-38-3. 184 pgs.

Praises in the Tushita Heaven, Chapter Twenty-four. Verses in praise of the Buddha spoken by the great Bodhisattvas after the Buddha arrived in the Tushita Heaven, prior to Vajra Banner Bodhisattva's explanation of the Ten Transferences.
ISBN 0-917512-39-1. 130 pgs.

Ten Grounds, Chapter Twenty-six, Part One. Contains the First Ground of Happiness, which focuses on the practice of giving.
ISBN 0-917512-87-1. 234 pgs.
Part Two. Covers the Bodhisattva's Second Ground of Leaving Filth, Third Ground of Emitting Light, and Fourth Ground of Blazing Wisdom. ISBN 0-917512-74-X. 200 pgs.

Universal Worthy's Conduct, Chapter Thirty-six. Universal Worthy Bodhisattva explains obstructions that arise from anger; gives methods to correct it when it does arise; and describes the purities, wisdoms, universal entrances, and supremely wondrous minds that result.
ISBN 0-88139-011-9. 75 pgs.

Entering the Dharma Realm, Chapter Thirty-nine. This chapter, which makes up one quarter of the entire Sutra, contains the spiritual journey of the Youth Good Wealth in his search for Ultimate Awakening. During his quest, he meets fifty-three Good Teachers, each of whom represents a successive stage on the Bodhisattva path. This is the first English translation of this chapter.

Universal Worthy's Conduct and Vows, Chapter Forty. A detailed explanation of Universal Worthy Bodhisattva's ten great kinds of practice, considered to be the foremost of all practices. ISBN 0-917512-84-7. 300 pgs.

Heart Sutra & Verses without a Stand. Considered the most popular Sutra in the world today, the text of the *Heart Sutra* explains the meaning of Prajna-paramita, the perfection of wisdom that is able to clearly perceive the emptiness of all phenomena. Each line in the text is accompanied by an eloquent verse by the Venerable Master Hsuan Hua and his commentary, which contains an explanation of most of the fundamental Buddhist concepts. ISBN 0-917512-27-8. 160 pgs. $7.50.

Shurangama Sutra. This Sutra gives the most detailed explanation of the Buddha's teachings concerning the mind. It includes an analysis of where the mind is located, an explanation of the origin of the cosmos, a discussion of the specific workings of *karma*, a description of all the realms of existence, and an exposition on the fifty kinds of deviant *samadhi*-concentrations, which can delude us in our search for awakening. Also, in this Sutra twenty-five enlightened sages explain the methods they used to become enlightened. This work will be eight volumes when completed. Set of first seven volumes $59.50.

> **Volume One.** The Venerable Ananda presents seven ideas on the location of the mind. The Buddha shows how each one is incorrect and then explains the roots of the false and the true. ISBN 0-917512-17-0. 289 pgs.

> **Volume Two.** The Buddha gives a clear description of the qualities of all the sense fields, their respective consciousnesses, and all the internal and external elemental forces of the universe. He explains how all are ultimately unreal, neither existing through causes nor arising spontaneously. ISBN 0-917512-25-1. 212 pgs.

Volume Three. The Buddha gives a clear description of the qualities of all the sense fields, their respective consciousnesses, and all the internal and external elemental forces of the universe. He explains how all are ultimately unreal, neither existing through causes nor arising spontaneously. ISBN 0-917512-94-4. 240 pgs.

Volume Four. The Buddha talks about the formation of the world, the coming into being of sentient creatures, and the cycle of karmic retribution. ISBN 0-917512-95-2. 200 pgs.

Volume Five. Twenty-five sages explain the method each used to transcend the realm of birth and death. Manjushri Bodhisattva selects the method used by the Bodhisattva Kuan Yin of "returning the hearing to listen to the self-nature" as the most appropriate for people in our world system. ISBN 0-917512-91-X. 250 pgs.

Volume Six. Includes the Buddha's explanation of the Four Clear and Unalterable Instructions on Purity, how to establish a Bodhimanda, the Shurangama Mantra and its wondrous functions, and the twelve categories of living beings. ISBN 0-917512-97-9. 200 pgs.

Volume Seven. Contains an explanation of the fifty-five stages of the Bodhisattva's path to Enlightenment and of how beings fall into the hells and turn in the realms of the ghosts, animals, people, immortals, *asuras,* and the various heavens.
ISBN 0-917512-93-6. 270 pgs.

Sixth Patriarch Sutra. One of the foremost scriptures of Ch'an Buddhism, this text describes the life and teachings of the remarkable Patriarch of the T'ang Dynasty, Great Master Hui Neng, who, though unable to read or write, was enlightened to the true nature of all things.
Softcover, ISBN 0-917512-19-7. 235 pgs. $10.00.
Hardcover, ISBN 0-917512-33-2. $15.00.

Sutra in Forty-two Sections. In this Sutra, which was the first to be transported from India and translated into Chinese, the Buddha gives the most essential instructions for cultivating the Dharma, emphasizing the cardinal virtues of renunciation, contentment, and patience. First edition, ISBN 0-917512-15-4. 114 pgs. $5.00. Second edition, hardcover, bilingual, ISBN 0-88139-184-0. 347 pgs. $12.00.

Sutra of the Past Vows of Earth Store Bodhisattva. This Sutra tells how Earth Store Bodhisattva attained his position among the greatest Bodhisattvas as the Foremost in Vows. It also explains the workings of *karma*, how beings undergo rebirth, and the various kinds of hells. This is the first English translation. Hardcover only, ISBN 0-917512-09-X. 235 pgs. $16.00. English text, without commentary, for recitation also available: ISBN 0-88139-502-1. 120 pgs. $7.00

Vajra Prajna Paramita (Diamond) Sutra. One of the most popular scriptures, the *Vajra Sutra* explains how the Bodhisattva relies on the perfection of wisdom to teach and transform beings.
ISBN 0-917512-02-2. 192 pgs. $8.00.

Commentarial Literature

Buddha Root Farm. A collection of lectures given during an Amitabha Buddha recitation session, explaining the practice and philosophy of the Pure Land School. The instructions are very thorough and especially useful for the beginner. ISBN 0-917512-08-1. 72 pgs. $4.00.

City of 10,000 Buddhas Recitation Handbook. Contains all the material covered in the traditional morning, afternoon, and evening services and special services recited daily in Buddhist monasteries in the East and West. Includes scriptures, praises, chants, mantras, repentances, and so forth. Bilingual edition. Chinese/English. ISBN 0-88139-167-0. 240 pgs. $7.00.

Filiality: The Human Source. Filiality is the very root of Way virtue. It is the single most vital force that sustains the universe. Therefore, it is only natural that Buddhist disciples base their conduct on an attitude of filial piety and respect for their parents and elders; for the rulers and officials of countries and the world; for the Triple Jewel; and ultimately for all living beings. All beings have at one time or another been our parents. Volumes I and II of this series contain stories from the twenty-four famous tales of filial paragons of China and numerous excerpts from Buddhist Sutras about filial behavior. Volume One, ISBN 0-88139-006-2, 120 pgs. $7.00. Volume Two, ISBN 0-88139-020-8. 120 pgs. $7.00.

Herein Lies the Treasure-trove. Various talks given by the Venerable Master at the City of 10,000 Buddhas.
Volume One, ISBN 0-88139-001-1. 250 pgs. $6.50.
Volume Two, ISBN 0-88139-115-8. 150 pgs. $6.50.

Listen to Yourself, Think Everything Over. Instructions on how to practice the method of reciting the names of the Buddhas and Bodhisattvas. Also includes a straightforward explanation of how to cultivate Ch'an meditation. All instructions were given during actual meditation and recitation sessions.
Volume One, ISBN 0-917512-24-3. 153 pgs. $7.00.
Volume Two, ISBN 0-88139-010-0. 200 pgs. $7.00.

Shastra on the Door to Understanding the Hundred Dharmas. A text fundamental to Consciousness Only doctrine, by Vasubandhu Bodhisattva, with commentary by the Venerable Master Hua. Includes lists of the Hundred Dharmas in English, Chinese, and Sanskrit for memorization. ISBN 0-88139-003-8. 130 pgs. $6.50.

Song of Enlightenment. The famous lyric poem of the state of the Ch'an sage, by the Venerable Master Yung Chia of the T'ang Dynasty. ISBN 0-88139-100-X. 85 pgs. $5.00.

The Ten Dharma Realms Are Not beyond a Single Thought. An eloquent poem on all the realms of being, accompanied by extensive commentarial material and drawings. ISBN 0-917512-12-X. 72 pgs. $4.00.

Venerable Master Hua's Talks on Dharma. Collections of talks given by the Venerable Master on various occasions. Emphasis is placed on how to apply Buddhist principles to personal cultivation. Bilingual Chinese/English.
Volume One, ISBN 0-88139-025-9. 227 pgs. $7.50.
Volume Two, ISBN 0-88139-026-7. 217 pgs. $7.50.
Volume Three, ISBN 0-88139-027-5. 219 pgs. $7.50.
Volume Four, ISBN 0-88139-028-3. 217 pgs. $7.50.

(**Khai Thi, Quyên 1.** Vietnamese translation of Volumes One & Two of *Venerable Master Hua's Talks on Dharma*, complete in one book. ISBN 0-88139-200-6. 264 pgs. $10.00.)

Venerable Master Hua's Talks on Dharma during the 1993 Trip to Taiwan. Special Edition of *Talks on Dharma* series. Talks given during the Vernerable Master's final visit to Taiwan. Bilingual Chinese/English. Fifteen pages of color photos. Glossary.
ISBN 0-88139-023-2. 279 pgs. $8.50.

Water Mirror Reflecting Heaven. An essay on the fundamental principle of cause and effect, with biographical material on contemporary Buddhist cultivation in China. Clear and to the point; very readable for young and old. ISBN 0-88139-501-3. 82 pgs. $4.00.

Biographical

In Memory of the Venerable Master Hsuan Hua. Compiled following Master Hua's "completion of the stillness" on June 7, 1995, these books contain photos of the Master and the programs he founded as well as biographical accounts of the Master's life, essays, and poems written by the Master's disciples and others whose lives he touched. Volume Two includes photos of the cremation ceremony and other memorial ceremonies. Both volumes are bilingual Chinese/English.
Volume One, hardcover, ISBN 0-88139-554-4. 249 pgs. $35.00
Volume Two, hardcover only, ISBN 0-88139-553-6. 506 pgs. $45.00.

Pictorial Biography of the Venerable Master Hsü Yün. Prose and verse written by the Venerable Master Hua documenting Venerable Yün's life. Illustrated with brush drawings. Each volume contains 104 sections of prose, verse, and drawings.
Volume One, ISBN 0-88139-008-9. 120 pgs.
Volume Two, ISBN 0-88139-116-6. Two volume set. $16.00.

Records of High Sanghans. A living tradition is sustained to the extent that it is embodied in its heroes. The Buddhist tradition is enhanced by a large body of literature containing truly moving and inspiring life stories of Sanghans (monastics) who dedicated their bodies and lives to the preservation and propagation of the Sagely Teachings. Volume One covers the life stories of the first eminent Sanghans who brought the Buddha-dharma from India to China and the adventures of those first Sanghans who withstood severe trials and hardships as they translated the first Sutras from Indian languages into Chinese. ISBN 0-88139-012-7. 158 pgs. $7.00.

Records of the Life of the Venerable Master Hsuan Hua. The life and teachings of the Venerable Master from his birth in China to the present time in America.

   Volume One. Covers the Venerable Master's life in China.
   ISBN 0-917512-78-2. 96 pgs. $5.00.
   (Spanish edition—Relaciones de la Vida del Maestro Hsuan Hua, Volume 1. ISBN 0-917512-31-6. 69 pgs. $8.00.)
   Volume Two. Covers the events of the Master's life as he cultivated and taught in Hong Kong. Contains many photos, poems, and stories.
   ISBN 0-917512-10-3. 229 pgs. $8.00.

Three Steps, One Bow. The daily journals of American Bhikshus Heng Ju and Heng Yo, who during 1973 and 1974 made a pilgrimage for world peace from Gold Mountain Monastery in San Francisco to Seattle, Washington, making a full prostration (kowtowing) every third step. The pilgrimage was inspired by monks in ancient China who would bow every third step for thousands of miles to a famous monastery or renowned teacher. ISBN 0-917512-18-9. 160 pgs. $5.00.

World Peace Gathering. A collection of instructional talks on Buddhism commemorating the successful completion of the bowing pilgrimage of Bhikshus Heng Ju and Heng Yo.
ISBN 0-917512-05-7. 128 pgs. $5.00.

News from True Cultivators. The letters written by the two more recent"Three Steps, One Bow" monks, Dharma Masters Heng Sure and Heng Ch'au, during their bowing pilgrimage, addressed to the Venerable Abbot and the Assembly of the City of Ten Thousand Buddhas, are uplifting messages to those traversing the path of cultivation and inspiring exhortations to all those concerned with evolving vital and workable methods to alleviate the acute problems of our troubled times. The language is simple; the insights are profound. No one should miss reading these books! Volume One, ISBN 0-88139-508-0. $6.00.
Volume Two, ISBN 0-88139-024-0. $6.00.

Open Your Eyes, Take a Look at the World. The journals of Bhikshus Heng Sure and Heng Ch'au and Bhikshuni Heng Tao, written during the 1978 Asia-region visit by the Venerable Master and other members of the Sino-American Buddhist Association.
ISBN 0-917512-32-4. 347 pgs. $9.00.

With One Heart Bowing to the City of 10,000 Buddhas. The moving journals of American Bhikshus Heng Sure and Heng Ch'au, who made a "Three Steps, One Bow" pilgrimage from Gold Wheel Temple in Los Angeles to the City of 10,000 Buddhas, located 110 miles north of San Francisco, from May 1977 to October 1979. Set $63.00.

Volume One. May 6–June 30, 1977.
ISBN 0-917512-21-9. 180 pgs.

Volume Two. July 1–October 30, 1977.
ISBN 0-917512-23-5. 322 pgs.

Volume Three. October 30–December 20, 1977.
ISBN 0-917512-89-8. 154 pgs.

Volume Four. December 17, 1977–January 21, 1978.
ISBN 0-917512-90-1. 136 pgs.

Volume Five. January 28–February 18, 1978.
ISBN 0-917512-91-X. 127 pgs.

Volume Six. February 19–April 2, 1978.
ISBN 0-917512-92-8. 200 pgs.

Volume Seven. April 3–May 24, 1978.
ISBN 0-917512-99-5. 160 pgs.

Volume Eight. May 24-September, 1978
ISBN 0-917512-53-7. 232 pgs.

Volume Nine. September–October, 1978.
ISBN 0-917512-509-9. 232 pgs.

If you would like to join in the volunteer work of the Buddhist Text Translation Society (computer typing, or whatever your talent), please contact:

The Buddhist Text Translation Society
1777 Murchison Drive
Burlingame, California 94010-4504
Phone (415) 692-5912; Fax (415) 692-5056

or your local branch of the Dharma Realm Buddhist Association.

中文佛經叢書名稱	冊數	版本	價格（美元）
大方廣佛華嚴經疏序淺釋（革新版）	1	平裝	$6.00
大方廣佛華嚴經淺釋	23	平裝	$173.00
大佛頂首楞嚴經淺釋	2	精裝	$40.00
大佛頂首楞嚴經大勢至菩薩念佛圓通章淺釋	1	平裝	$7.00
大佛頂首楞嚴經五十陰魔淺釋	1	精裝	$32.00
大佛頂首楞嚴經四種清淨明誨淺釋	1	平裝	$5.00
楞伽經會譯	4	平裝	$24.00
觀楞伽阿跋多羅寶經記	6	平裝	$36.00
楞伽經註	2	平裝	$12.00
大乘妙法蓮華經淺釋	4	平裝	$40.00
妙法蓮華經觀世音菩薩普門品淺釋	1	平裝	$6.00
妙法蓮華經安樂行品淺釋	1	精裝	$18.00
金剛般若波羅蜜經淺釋	1	平裝	$7.00
金剛般若波羅蜜經淺釋	1	精裝	$15.00
般若波羅蜜多心經非台頌解（革新版）	1	平裝	$6.00
六祖法寶壇經淺釋	1	平裝	$8.00
永嘉大師證道歌淺釋	1	平裝	$6.00
楞嚴咒（袖珍本）	1	摺疊本	$4.00
楞嚴咒疏	1	平裝	$10.00

中文佛經叢書名稱	冊數	版本	價格
			（美元）
佛說阿彌陀經淺釋	1	精裝	$12.00
地藏菩薩本願經淺釋	1	精裝	$12.00
地藏菩薩本願經淺釋	3	精裝	$25.00
誌公禪師因果經	1	精裝	$12.00
藥師琉璃光如來本願功德經淺釋	1	精裝	$20.00
佛說四十二章經淺釋	1	精裝	$11.50
佛遺教經淺釋	2	平裝	$16.00
梵網經菩薩戒本	1	平裝	$10.00
梵網經講錄（中英版）	2	平裝	$50.00
梵網經菩薩戒本持犯集證類編	1	平裝	$3.00
沙彌律儀要略解合訂本	1	平裝	$8.00
學佛行儀、五戒表解合訂本	1	平裝	$6.00
大乘百法明門論淺釋	1	平裝	$6.00
大乘起信論	1	平裝	$6.00
禪海十珍	1	平裝	$8.00
佛祖道影	4	線裝	$50.00
虛雲老和尚畫傳集（中英版）	1	精裝	$15.00
虛雲老和尚畫傳集（中英版）	2	平裝	$16.00
虛雲老和尚年譜	1	平裝	$6.00
宣化上人事蹟（革新版）	1	平裝	$20.00

中文佛經叢書名稱	冊數	版本	價格（美元）
萬佛聖城日誦儀規（革新版）	1	平裝	$7.00
大悲懺本（中英版）	1	平裝	$4.00
初一、十五佛前大供	1	平裝	$5.00
宣化上人開示錄全集（六冊合訂）	2	精裝	$40.00
宣化上人開示錄（五冊合訂）	2	精裝	$35.00
宣化上人開示錄	6	平裝	$36.00
宣化上人開示錄（一九九三年訪臺開示）	1	平裝	$7.50
人生要義（革新版）	1	平裝	$8.00
歐洲弘法記	1	平裝	$8.00
水鏡回天錄	2	精裝	$24.00
人之根（注音革新版）	1	平裝	$8.00
十法界不離一念心	1	平裝	$7.00
參禪要旨	1	平裝	$7.00
虛雲老和尚開示	1	平裝	$7.00
修行者的消息	2	平裝	$14.40
佛教精進者的日記（一）革新版	1	平裝	$8.00
佛教精進者的日記（二）革新版	1	平裝	$8.00
佛教精進者的日記（三）革新版	1	平裝	$7.00
中國文學選讀	1	精裝	$20.00

中英雙語對照叢書 **Bilingual Chinese/English** **Buddhist Books**	冊數 **No. of** **Vols.**	版本 **Edition**	價格 （美元） **Price**
楞嚴經五十陰魔淺釋 The Shurangama Sutra: The Fifty Skandha-Demon States	1	精裝中英版 English/Chinese	**$35.00**
佛說四十二章經淺釋 The Sutra in Forty-two Sections Spoken by the Buddha	1	精裝中英版 English/Chinese	**$12.00**
宣化上人開示錄（一） Venerable Master Hua's Talks on Dharma, Vol. 1	1	平裝中英版 English/Chinese	**$7.50**
宣化上人開示錄（二） Venerable Master Hua's Talks on Dharma, Vol. 2	1	平裝中英版 English/Chinese	**$7.50**
宣化上人開示錄（三） Venerable Master Hua's Talks on Dharma, Vol. 3	1	平裝中英版 English/Chinese	**$7.50**
宣化上人開示錄（四） Venerable Master Hua's Talks on Dharma, Vol. 4	1	平裝中英版 English/Chinese	**$7.50**

宣化上人開示錄
（一九九三年訪臺開示）
Venerable Master Hua's
  Talks on Dharma during the
  1993 Trip to Taiwan
	1	平裝中英版
		English/Chinese
			$10.00

中英雙語對照叢書 Bilingual Chinese/English Buddhist Books	册數 No. of Vols.	版本 Edition	價格 （美元） Price
宣化老和尚追思紀念專集（一） In Memory of the Venerable Master Hsuan Hua Volume One	1	精裝中英版 English/Chinese	$35.00
宣化老和尚追思紀念專集（二） In Memory of the Venerable Master Hsuan Hua Volume Two	1	精裝中英版 English/Chinese	$45.00

錄音帶品名	語言	卷數	包裝	價格 （美元）
大佛頂首楞嚴經淺釋	中文	120*	盒裝	$320.00
大佛頂首楞嚴經 　四種清淨明誨淺釋	中文	4*	盒裝	$15.00
大方廣佛華嚴經 　普賢行願品淺釋	中文	18*	盒裝	$40.00
大方廣佛華嚴經淨行品淺釋	中文	12	盒裝	$40.00
大方廣佛華嚴經疏序淺釋	中文	8*	盒裝	$25.00
六祖法寶壇經淺釋	中文	24*	盒裝	$60.00
金剛般若波羅蜜經淺釋	中文	14*	盒裝	$35.00
佛說阿彌陀經淺釋	中文	14	盒裝	$45.00

* 附書

錄音帶品名	語言	卷數	包裝	價格 (美元)
佛說四十二章經淺釋	中文	6*	盒裝	$23.00
佛遺教經淺釋	中文	9*	盒裝	$30.00
般若波羅蜜多心經非台頌解	中文	8*	盒裝	$25.00
大乘百法明門論淺釋	中文	5*	盒裝	$20.00
妙法蓮華經安樂行品淺釋	中文	9	盒裝	$30.00
妙法蓮華經 　觀世音菩薩普門品淺釋	中文	15	盒裝	$30.00
藥性賦	中文	5	盒裝	$18.00
觀音菩薩的智慧鑰匙	中文	4	盒裝	$15.00
禪(開示)	中文	3	盒裝	$12.00
佛七精華錄	中文	5	盒裝	$18.00
佛陀十大弟子傳	中文	3	盒裝	$12.00
十法界不離一念心	中文	3	盒裝	$12.00
念佛法門到彼岸	中文	3	盒裝	$12.00
高僧傳	中文	22	盒裝	$70.00
救世界教育的靈丹	中文	3	盒裝	$12.00
楞嚴咒	中文	1	單片	$5.00
大悲咒	中文	1	單片	$5.00
大悲懺	中文	1	單片	$7.00
觀世音菩薩聖號	中文	1	單片	$5.00

＊ 附書

錄音帶品名	語言	卷數	包裝	價格 (美元)
正法的震撼 　一九八八年臺灣弘法專集	中文	12	盒裝	$30.00
宣化上人開示錄(一) 　一九八八年馬來西亞弘法專集	中文	4	盒裝	$12.00
宣化上人開示錄(二) 　美加地區等弘法結集	中文	6	盒裝	$18.00
宣化上人開示錄(三)	台語	4	盒裝	$12.00
宣化上人開示錄(四) 　一九八九年臺灣弘法專集	中文	7	盒裝	$21.00
宣化上人開示錄(五) 　一九九〇年臺灣弘法專集	中文	6	盒裝	$18.00
宣化上人開示錄(六) 　一九九三年訪臺開示	中文	5	盒裝	$18.00
宣化上人開示錄 　一九九四年於美國	中文	7	單片	$5.00
宣化上人開示錄	粵語	16	單片	$5.00

* 附書

錄影帶品名	卷數	價格 (美元)
智慧光	6	$150.00
修行在聖城	1	$15.00
南傳北傳大團結	1	$15.00
傳戒在聖城	1	$15.00

錄音帶品名 **AUDIO TAPES** Title	語言 Language	卷數 # of Tapes	包裝 Set / Single Tape	價格 Price US$
宣化上人開示錄（一九九四年） Venerable Master Hua's Talks on Dharma (1994)	中英 Bilingual	12	單片 single	$5.00
佛說四十二章經淺釋 The Sutra in Forty-two Sections Spoken by the Buddha	中英 Bilingual	10	盒裝 set	$32.00

宣化上人開示錄（1993年訪臺開示）
Venerable Master Hua's
  Talks on Dharma during the
  1993 Trip to Taiwan
	中英
	Bilingual
		6	盒裝
			set
				$21.00

正法的代表 A Sure Sign of the Proper Dharma	中英 Bilingual	2*	盒裝 set	$15.00
百年大事渾如夢 The Great Events of One Hundred Years Are Hazy As If a Dream	中英 Bilingual	1*	盒裝 set	$10.00
皈依的真義 The True Meaning of Taking Refuge	中英 Bilingual	1*	盒裝 set	$10.00
Guanyin Bodhisattva Is Our Brother	English	1	single	$5.00
The Patriarch Bodhidharma's Advent in China	English	1	single	$5.00
On Investigating a Meditation Topic	English	1	single	$5.00
The State of Chan Meditation	English	1	single	$5.00
Both Good and Evil Exist in a Single Thought	English	1	single	$5.00
Cultivate Merit and Virtue without Marks	English	1	single	$5.00

with pocket-size book 附書

Vajra Bodhi Sea

Vajra Bodhi Sea is a monthly journal of orthodox Buddhism which has been published by the Dharma Realm Buddhist Association, formerly known as the Sino-American Buddhist Association, since 1970. Each issue contains the most recent translations of the Buddhist canon by the Buddhist Text ranslation Society. Also included in each issue are a biography of a great Patriarch of Buddhism from the ancient past, sketches of the lives of contemporary monastics and lay-followers around the world, articles on practice, and other material. The journal is bilingual, Chinese and English, 48 pages in an 8½" by 11" format. ISSN 0507-6986. Single issues, $4.00. One year subscription, $40.00; three years, $100.00. (Postage is included in the subscription fee.) Send orders to:

Vajra Bodhi Sea subscriptions
800 Sacramento Street
San Francisco, CA 94108
(415) 421-6117

月刊	版本	價格（美元）
萬佛聖城月刊金剛菩提海雜誌 單行本	中英版	$4.00
萬佛聖城月刊金剛菩提海雜誌 訂閱一年	中英版	$40.00
萬佛聖城月刊金剛菩提海雜誌 訂閱二年	中英版	$75.00
萬佛聖城月刊金剛菩提海雜誌 訂閱三年	中英版	$100.00

Ordering Information 郵購須知

Postage & Handling 郵費及手續費:
The following rates for postage and handling apply to orders of six or fewer books. Up to six audio tapes count as one book. On orders of more than six books, we suggest that purchasers submit their orders for a precise quote on postage and handling costs.
每六片錄音帶照一本書計費。郵購不足六本書,照下列計費法:
郵購超過六本,請將郵購單寄至上列地址估計費用。

    United States: $2.00 for the first book and $0.75 for each additional book. All publications are sent via special fourth class. Allow from two weeks to one month for delivery.

    International: $2.50 for the first book and $1.50 for each additional book. All publications are sent via "book rate" or direct mail sack (surface). For countries in which parcels may be lost, we suggest orders be sent via registered mail for an additional $3.25 per parcel of ten books each. We are not responsible for parcels lost in the mail. Allow two to three months for delivery.

美國境內:若購買一本書$2.00美元。二本書以上每冊$0.75美元。以四級郵遞,需時兩星期至一個月。

美國境外:若購買一本書$2.50美元,二本書以上每冊$1.25美元。陸運。郵遞容易遺失之地,請掛號郵寄:每包十本書另加郵資$3.75美元。郵件若有遺失,本會不負任何責任。郵遞時間需時二至三個月。

■California residents add 8.25% tax. 加州居民另加上8.25%之稅金。
■Make checks payable to: D.R.B.A. 支票抬頭請寫D.R.B.A.
All orders require prepayment, including postage and handling fees, before they will be shipped to the buyer. Submit order to:
郵購請先付款,包括郵費及手續費。郵購單請寄:

    Buddhist Text Translation Society 佛經翻譯委員會
    Sagely City of Ten Thousand Buddhas 萬佛聖城
    2001 Talmage Road, P.O. Box 217, Talmage, CA 95481-0217 U.S.A.
    Phone電話: (707) 462-0939; Fax傳真: (707) 462-0949

             or to 或:

    Buddhist Text Translation Society 佛經翻譯委員會
    International Translation Institute 國際譯經學院
    1777 Murchison Drive, Burlingame, CA 94010-4504 U.S.A.
    Phone電話: (415) 692-5912; Fax傳真: (415) 692-5056

Most branches of the Dharma Realm Buddhist Association, as well as some retail booksellers, also offer Buddhist Text Translation Society publications for sale.
錄音帶及書籍於法界佛教總會所屬道場,及有些書局,均可請得。

ORDER FORM 訂購單

Name 姓名:＿＿＿＿＿＿＿＿＿＿＿＿

Address 地址:＿＿＿＿＿＿＿＿＿＿

＿＿＿＿＿＿＿＿＿＿＿＿＿＿＿＿

＿＿＿＿＿＿＿＿＿＿＿＿＿

五本以上打九折，大量訂購請來電洽商。
10% discount for five or more books
please call or write for discounts on quantity orders

Title 項目	Qty 數量	Amount 金額
(Calif. residents, 8.25% tax 加州居民另加上稅金)		
postage and handling 郵購費:		
Total 總額:		

法界佛教總會 · 萬佛聖城
Dharma Realm Buddhist Association
The City of Ten Thousand Buddhas
2001 Talmage Road, Talmage, CA 95481-0217 U.S.A.
Tel: (707) 462-0939   Fax: (707) 462-0949

法界聖城 **The City of the Dharma Realm**
1029 West Capitol Ave., West Sacramento, CA 95691 U.S.A.
Tel: (916) 374-8268

國際譯經學院 **The International Translation Institute**
1777 Murchison Drive, Burlingame, CA 94010 U.S.A.
Tel: (415) 692-5912

法界宗教研究院
Institute for World Religions (at Berkeley Buddhist Monastery)
2304 McKinley Avenue, Berkeley, CA 94703 U.S.A.
Tel: (510) 848-3440

金山聖寺 **Gold Mountain Monastery**
800 Sacramento Street, San Francisco, CA 94108 U.S.A.
Tel: (415) 421-6117

金輪聖寺 **Gold Wheel Monastery**
235 N. Avenue 58, Los Angeles, CA 90042 U.S.A.
Tel: (213) 258-6668

長堤聖寺 **Long Beach Monastery**
3361 East Ocean Boulevard, Long Beach, CA 90803 U.S.A.
Tel: (310) 438-8902

福祿壽聖寺 **Blessing, Prosperity, & Longevity Monastery**
4140 Long Beach Boulevard, Long Beach, CA 90807 U.S.A.
Tel: (310) 595-4966

華嚴精舍 **Avatamasaka Hermitage**
11721 Beall Mountain Road, Potomac, MD 20854 U.S.A.
Tel: (301) 299-3693

金聖寺 **Gold Sage Monastery**
11455 Clayton Road, San Jose, CA 95127 U.S.A.
Tel: (408) 923-7243

金峰聖寺 **Gold Summit Monastery**
233-1st Ave. West, Seattle, WA 98119 U.S.A.
Tel: (206) 217-9320

金佛聖寺 **Gold Buddha Monastery**
301 East Hastings Street, Vancouver, BC, V6A 1P3 Canada.
Tel: (604) 684-3754

華嚴聖寺 **Avatamsaka Monastery**
1152 10th Street SE, Calgary, AB, T2G 3E4 Canada.
Tel: (403) 269-2960

法界佛教印經會
Dharma Realm Buddhist Books Distribution Association
臺北市忠孝東路六段85號11樓
11th Floor, 85 Chung-hsiao E. Road, Sec. 6, Taipei, R.O.C.
Tel: (02) 786-3022

紫雲洞觀音寺 **Tze Yun Tung Temple**
Batu 5½, Jalan Sungai Besi, Salak Selatan,
57100 Kuala Lumpur, Malaysia.
Tel: (03) 782-6560

佛教講堂 **Buddhist Lecture Hall**
31 Wong Nei Chong Road, Top Floor, Happy Valley, HONG KONG.
香港跑馬地黃泥涌道31號12樓
Tel: 2572-7644

十法界不離一念心

西曆一九九六年六月二十五日・中英文版
佛曆三〇二三年五月初十・宣公上人涅槃紀念日・初版

發 行 人	法界佛教總會	
督 印	宣化上人	
出 版	法界佛教總會/佛經翻譯委員會/法界佛教大學	
地 址	1777 Murchison Drive	
	Burlingame, CA 94010-4504 U.S.A.	
電 話	(415) 692-5912	
倡 印	萬佛聖城	
地 址	2001 Talmage Road	
	Talmage, CA 95481-0217 U.S.A.	
電 話	(707) 462-0939	

ISBN-0-88139-503-x